CANADIANS —IN THE WINTER OLYMPICS

J. Alexander Poulton

OVER TIME BOOKS

Thompson-Nicola Regional District
Library System
300-465 VICTORIA STREET
KAMLOOPS, BC   V2C 2A9

© 2009 by OverTime Books
First printed in 2009 10 9 8 7 6 5 4 3 2 1
Printed in Canada

The Publisher: OverTime Books is an imprint of Éditions de la Montagne Verte

Library and Archives Canada Cataloguing in Publication

Poulton, J. Alexander (Jay Alexander), 1977–
    Canadians at the Winter Olympics / J. Alexander Poulton.

Includes bibliographical references.
ISBN 978-1-897277-38-6

    1. Athletes—Canada—Biography. 2. Olympics—Participation, Canadian. I. Title.

GV697.A1P668 2009   796.480971   C2008-906185-3

Project Director: J. Alexander Poulton
Editor: Kathy van Denderen
Cover Image: ©Diademimages | Dreamstime.com (Eric Bedard of Canada in Turin, Italy, 2006)

We acknowledge the financial support of the Government of Canada through the Book Publishing Industry Development Program for our publishing activities.

	Canadian	Patrimoine
	Heritage	canadien

PC: 6

Contents

Introduction 5

Chapter 1:
A Look Ahead to 2010 Vancouver . . . 12

Chapter 2:
**2010 Vancouver Olympics: A Look
at the Numbers** 17

Chapter 3:
The Canadian Game 20

Chapter 4:
Figure Skating 83

Chapter 5:
Speed Skating 116

Chapter 6:
Snow Sports 145

Chapter 7:
**On the Ice: Curling, Bobsled, Skeleton
and Luge** 196

Chapter 8:
Quick Facts and Stats 215

Notes on Sources 246

Dedication

To Claudette and Jeff

Introduction

We are a nation that loves its hockey. It goes almost without saying. Ask people from around the world what Canada is best known for, and most would answer with hockey, along with snow, Mounties and beavers. But we are more than hockey. We are six-time Olympic medallist speed skating Cindy Klassen; three-time Olympic biathlete Myriam Bedard; figure skating sweetheart Elizabeth Manley; and five-time short track speed skating medallist Marc Gagnon. From the very first Winter Olympics in 1924 to the Games in 2010 in Vancouver, Canada's best amateur (with the occasional pro) athletes have given all of themselves in pursuit of the Olympic dream. Statistically, it is a losing prospect to come away with an Olympic medal, but our athletes have always remained undaunted by the difficult tasks in front of them and, win or lose, they have provided us with moments that will last forever, such as Nancy

Greene's double-medal performance in the downhill event at the 1968 Winter Games in Grenoble, France.

Off the slopes and onto the track, one of the greatest moments in Canadian bobsled history came out of the 1964 Games in Innsbruck, Austria, when Vic Emery gathered together a group of athletes and decided to give Olympic gold their best shot. Vic, his brother John, and friends Peter Kirby and Doug Anakin were relatively unknown Canadians who stepped onto the track and blew away the competition to win Canada's first gold medal, or any medal for that matter, in Olympic bobsleigh. It took another 34 years before Canada was back on the centre podium in Olympic bobsleigh competition, when Dave MacEachern and Pierre Lueders won gold at the 1998 Games in Nagano, Japan, in the two-man event.

The Olympics have been filled with incredible surprise moments. Those of us old enough to remember can never forget the look on Elizabeth Manley's face as she came to a halt at centre ice in the Calgary Saddledome in 1988 when she realized that she had just performed a flawless routine and had assured herself a medal. As much as she surprised the world, the look on her face after finishing her medal routine seemed to say she was the most surprised of all.

For those a little longer in the tooth, they will also remember Canada's first non-hockey gold medallist, the ever-graceful figure skater Barbara Ann Scott.

Going into the 1948 Olympics, Canada was more than aware of Scott's incredible grace and athleticism on the ice. Her legend was solidified in the year before the Games of 1948 when she became the first North American to win both the European and World Figure Skating titles. Scott was treated like a national hero, and her hometown of Ottawa wanted to give her a brand new convertible car for her exploits, but she had to turn the gift down in order to still be considered an amateur for the upcoming Olympic Games. Scott blew away the competition at the 1948 Olympics to capture Canada's first gold medal in Olympic figure skating singles history.

Individual Canadian athletes have had incredible success at the Games, but when grouped together as a team, Canada has proven to be a formidable force. Without a question, our nation's strongest team event has been hockey. In the first half of the history of the Winter Olympics, Canada was clearly the dominant force in the hockey world, producing five gold medals by the 1952 Games. But given enough time, the rest of the world caught on to the game of hockey and began producing teams that could not only challenge but also dominate the amateur players that Canada sent to the Games.

The one team that stood out was the Soviets. Closed off from the rest of the world, the Soviet Red Army team was able to develop and train highly "professional" hockey players who in time easily rivalled the "amateur" Canadians. The issue of the "professional"

Russian players bothered Canadian hockey officials to such a degree that they removed the national team from competition for the 1972 and 1976 Games in protest. The team returned for the 1980 Olympics in Lake Placid, New York, but it wasn't until the 1992 games in Albertville, France, that Canada would once again bring home a medal. It wasn't a gold, but it signalled the return of Team Canada to international competition. It took 10 years before the Canadian hockey professionals returned home with a gold medal around their necks, in 2002. Almost 50 years to the day after Canada last won Olympic gold in 1952, team captain Mario Lemieux led his team of Canadian NHL all-stars past some very difficult challenges, but their determination was too strong, and the gold medal was once again ours.

Since entering the Olympics in 1998, the Canadian women's hockey team has faired a little better than their male counterparts. When women's hockey finally got off the ground in the early 1990s, Canadian women were at the top of the class. Playing against countries such as Sweden, Finland and Russia, Canadian women repeatedly trounced the competition. The only team that seemed to give the Canadians any trouble was the Americans. By the late 1990s, the Americans were just as good as the Canadian women and were hungering for some revenge for those early years. Then came the 1998 Olympics in Nagano, Japan. This marked the first time that women's hockey would be part of the full Olympic program, and a gold medal would give the winner lifelong bragging rights. As fate would have it, the Canadians ended up facing the Americans in the final for the gold medal. The win was all the more pressing for the Canadian women because the men's team had been knocked off the podium completely. All the pressure seemed to throw Canada off their game, and the United States ended up winning the first gold medal in women's hockey. Four years later, however, Canada's team had its revenge.

Canadians have always seemed to excel in sports on ice, and the women's curling team that was sent to the 1998 Nagano Games led by skip Sandra Schmirler was one of our best. The three-time Canadian Champion and three-time World Champion won the right to represent Canada's curling team in Nagano, the first time curling was recognized as a full medal sport. There was some tough competition along the way, but Schmirler managed to pull off dramatic wins each time. Having a gold medal around her neck while the Canadian anthem played was probably the best moment of Sandra Schmirler's curling career. Unfortunately, her career in the sport was cut short when she contracted a deadly form of cancer and died just two years later. The legacy she left behind by her amazing performance at the Games will live on forever.

It is moments like these and many more that keep us waiting in anticipation for the next Olympics that will take Canadian between February 12 and 28, 2010, in the wonderful city of Vancouver. Although many might claim that the Olympics is just a collection of sports, the Games provide more than pure enjoyment on one level—through the athletes' trials and tribulations we get to view real human drama play out before our eyes. It is incredible to watch as athletes pour their heart and soul into their sport, working up to that singular moment in time when they compete with the world's best, and whether they win or lose, that very moment is the culmination of several years of sweat, tears and passion. To say that there is nothing interesting in watching athletes such as ours is to miss the whole point of what the Olympics is about.

Some of the top Canadians vying for Olympic gold in 2010 in Vancouver will be speed skating star Cindy Klassen, who is looking to add to her already incredible total of six Olympic medals. She has suffered a few setbacks since her domination of the 2006 Olympics, but the speedy Canadian is determined to score a few wins in front of the partisan audience. Equally looking to make a splash on the Olympic oval will be perennial favourite Jeremy Wotherspoon, who has won only one medal in three Olympic appearances despite dominating the World Championships. It is a frustrating fact for the Alberta native, but the extra incentive to win at the Vancouver Olympics was just too good to pass up.

Other Canadians hoping for a trip to the podium in Vancouver are Olympic bobsleigh veteran Pierre Lueders, veteran snowboarder Jasey-Jay Anderson, alpine skiers Erik Guay and Emily Brydon, skeleton driver Melissa Hollingsworth, figure skating hopefuls Patrick Chan and Joannie Rochette and a whole host of other young Canadian athletes looking to shine in front of the home crowd.

Canadians will no doubt be cheering on these individual athletes, but the most widely anticipated event of the 2010 Games is without a doubt hockey. For both the men's and women's teams it will not only be about proving to the world that hockey is Canada's game and that our players are the best, but it will also be about doing so on home ice. Expectations are always high, but they have attained new heights since it was announced that Vancouver would host the Olympics. The Canadian men and women who will be going into battle will face a tough challenge from their international counterparts, but with the noise level that will surely rise from the crowd, it will be tough to compete against that kind of advantage. This author, like most Canadians, will surely be watching as our men and women put in their best performances and show the world what real Canadians are made of.

Chapter One

A Look Ahead to 2010 Vancouver

Official Mission Statement of the 2010 Winter Olympics:

To touch the soul of the nation and inspire the world by creating and delivering an extraordinary Olympic and Paralympic experience with lasting legacies.

Vision:

A stronger Canada whose spirit is raised by its passion for sport, culture and sustainability.

On July 3, 2003, the city of Vancouver learned that it had won the honour of hosting the 2010 Winter Olympics, sending 10,000 hopeful citizens gathered at GM Place Stadium into a screaming frenzy. Just moments before the announcement, the entire stadium sat in unnerving silence as International Olympic Committee president Jacques Rogge took the podium to declare the winner. Vancouver had put in a strong bid for the Games, but there was some tough competition. Salzburg, Austria, and Pyeongchan,

South Korea, along with Vancouver, were the cities in the final round of selections, and through the first rounds of voting it looked as though Vancouver would lose their bid. But when Salzburg was eliminated, Vancouver knew that its chances were far better, as voters were less likely to hand an international event to a city whose neighbour had recently reported acquiring a nuclear weapon. But the voting was still close. The Games of the XXI Winter Olympiad were won by a mere three votes, 56–53. After the celebratory party ended, the city started plans to lay out its welcome mat for the world. But right from the start, questions arose about whether the city could pull off such an event.

The list of initial worries was long. Because Vancouver is the wettest and warmest city ever to host the Winter Games, there were concerns that there wouldn't be enough snow and ice on the ground for the events. Coastal weather is extremely unpredictable and, at times in February, Vancouver and the surrounding area look more like a rainforest than a winter wonderland. Vancouver Olympic officials also had to contend with an active and environmentally aware public who would be sensitive to the need to build a bobsled/luge/ skeleton run on the face of Blackcomb Mountain. But most controversial of all was the construction of a new highway between Vancouver and Whistler.

New stadiums would have to be built, as well as housing for the athletes, and the infrastructure had to be updated, which was estimated to cost $2.5 billion. The issue of the growing homeless population in the city was another worry. Attracted to the city's warm winter weather, Vancouver's homeless threatened to tarnish the city's reputation in front of the world.

The planning committee knew it would have a tough time convincing everyone that the Olympics would benefit all Vancouverites, but once the Games got underway, it was believed that hearts and minds would undoubtedly be swayed. The citizens of Vancouver might take a little longer to persuade, but the rest of Canada had jumped on board, and preparations began immediately to "Own the Podium."

When it was announced that Vancouver would host the 2010 Olympics, a movement arose between public and private partners called "Own the Podium." The movement has basically one goal: to win medals. Canada holds the dubious distinction of being the only host nation to have never won a gold medal: in Montréal in 1976 and in Calgary in 1988. It was almost understandable that Canada did not win at the Summer Games in Montréal, but to miss bringing in a gold medal at the Winter Games in Calgary was a true disappointment. Canada is, after all, the Great White North, and not winning a gold medal on home turf was a hard pill to swallow for the Canadian Olympic program.

Millions of dollars are needed to provide Olympic athletes with extra training, access to equipment, trainers and, most importantly, an open door to all the venues months prior to the start of the Games. The latter is incredibly important when looking at the alpine ski events, where Canadian athletes will be privy months in advance to every little bump, curve and jump on each run. This is not considered cheating; other host countries have done the same with some successes, so why not Canada? The Canadian athletes competing in the bobsleigh, luge and skeleton events will also have a greater advantage as they will be able to practice on the actual runs used come Olympic race day.

With these measures in place, the Canadian Olympic planners have set the lofty goal of beating its total medal haul of 24 at the Turin Olympics in 2006. Getting 24 medals or more should not be a problem for Canada's athletes; that is, if the weather cooperates. With all the Olympic venues ready, the only worry left for officials is whether Mother Nature will send some good weather the city's way. Vancouverites spend most of their winters laughing at the rest of Canada as it is buried in snow and extreme cold, but in 2010 they are praying Old Man Winter comes their way.

The weather factor is most important in Whistler Blackcomb, where the alpine skiing events will take place. When conditions are at their best, Whistler Blackcomb is one of the world's premiere ski destinations, but when hit with warm weather, the area can be downright miserable for skiers. Sitting at a relatively low elevation in the Rockies, Whistler Blackcomb's proximity to the salt water of the Pacific Ocean makes it vulnerable to occasional mid-winter warm spells that pour rain over the lower elevations of the mountain and cover the top in thick fog. This would spell disaster for the alpine, freestyle and cross-country skiing events. All Vancouver Olympic officials can do is hope and pray and have a solid set of contingency plans to fall back on.

Every Olympic Games, summer or winter, has its set of challenges to face, and the 2010 Games in Vancouver has already faced a few. But once the world descends on the city, they will no doubt discover a place and a people welcoming them with open arms for a party like none they have ever experienced, Canadian style!

Chapter Two

2010 Vancouver Olympics: A Look at the Numbers

City population: 2.3 million (metro area)

Olympic Winter Games dates: February 12 to 28, 2010

Paralympic Winter Games dates: March 12 to 21, 2010

Number of Olympic Games athletes and officials: 5500

Number of Paralympic Games athletes and officials: 1350

Number of countries participating in Olympic Winter Games: 80+

Number of countries participating in Paralympic Games: 40+

Estimated media representatives: 10,000

Estimated television viewers: 3 billion

Ticket Information

Available tickets: 1.6 million

Ticket prices (face value)

Opening ceremony: $175 to $1100

Alpine skiing: $120 to $150

Cross-country skiing/biathlon: $25 to $75

Bobsleigh/luge/skeleton: $30 to $85

Curling: $65 to $125

Figure skating: $50 to $525

Freestyle skiing: $50 to $125

Hockey: $25 to $775

Short-track speed skating: $50 to $150

Ski jumping: $80 to $210

Snowboarding: $50 to $150

Speed skating: $95 to $185

Closing ceremony: $175 to $775

New Event: Ski Cross

A relatively new type of skiing competition, ski cross is basically motor cross on snow. The course is a deadly mix of naturally occurring bumps and jumps and also any artificial features that the course designers can conjure up. Masses of skiers are sent hurdling down the treacherous course at speeds in excess of 70 kilometres per hour, and basically the first across the line wins. Any pulling or grabbing of other competitors is strictly prohibited, but bumping and crashes are inevitable.

Symbols and Mascots of the 2010 Vancouver Olympic Games

Every Olympic Games has an official mascot or mascots that are created to represent the culture and goodwill of the host nation. For the 2010 Vancouver Olympics, the organizing committee chose to feature symbols from the culture of the Aboriginal people of British Columbia.

Symbol of the Games

Ilaanaq the Inunnguag: This symbol is a stone statue made of piled rocks that resembles an inukshuk. *Ilaanaq* is a Native word for "friend."

Mascots

Miga: a mythical sea bear that is part orca and part bear

Quatchi: a sasquatch

Sumi (the Paralympic Games mascot): an animal guardian spirit with thunderbird wings and the legs of a black bear

Chapter Three

The Canadian Game

When the very first rules of hockey were being devised and the first teams began to hit the ice, little did the creators realize that they were developing a game that would grow into the most popular sport in Canada and in other countries around the world. But in Canada, hockey has become more than just a sport for entertainment's sake; the game has become part of our culture, part of our national language by which we define ourselves.

By the time the Winter Olympics officially began in 1924, Canada had already had over half a century of practice on the rest of the world and it dominated in the early years of the Olympics. From the 1920 Summer Games (yes, ice hockey in summer) to the 1952 Winter Games, Canada pretty much enjoyed complete control over the hockey world. Those years provided some great moments in the annals of Canadian hockey, but soon the world caught up, and Canada found it much harder to win games. Since the 1952 Games in Oslo, there have been some lean years, but hockey is still Canada's game, and it will always remain that way. The following sections in this chapter tell some of the greatest stories, both the good and the bad, of our men's and women's national teams on the ice.

Ice Hockey at the 1920 Summer Olympics

It has gone down in the history books that Canada's first gold medal in Olympic ice hockey was won at the first-ever Winter Olympics in Chamonix, France, in 1924, but technically, Canada won its first ice hockey gold at the 1920 Summer Olympics in Belgium.

The Winnipeg Falcons had just come off an incredible season in the Senior Amateur Hockey League, winning the Allan Cup Championship. After their display of superior hockey skills, the International Olympic Committee (IOC) invited the team to join their fellow Canadian athletes at the 1920 Olympics in Antwerp, Belgium. It did seem a little unusual that an ice hockey team was being invited to compete in the Summer Games, but the IOC had also invited figure skaters to the Games, so it appeared that the IOC was pushing to open a new winter version of the Games.

Getting the team to Belgium was not an easy task in the days before air travel. The total cost of the voyage from Canada to Antwerp was estimated at $10,000, a huge sum of money that was collected from municipal and provincial governments. From Winnipeg, the Falcons travelled to Toronto, Ottawa, then to Montréal, where a few members of the Montréal AAA (Amateur Athletic Association) joined the team. A few days later they were back on a train and headed to Saint John, New Brunswick, where they boarded the SS *Melita* for the one-week voyage across the Atlantic. It was a relatively uneventful trip, but the ship's carpenter took the time to carve two dozen hockey sticks from some rough wood the players had obtained in Montréal. At that time, hockey sticks were not yet mass-produced, and players preferred to use a stick that was made to their specific needs and tastes. These were the only sticks the players used during the entire 1920 Olympics.

The rules of the game called for the seven-man version of hockey, which included the position of a rover. The rover did not really have a set position but instead skated to the part of the ice that needed him the most. This system of hockey was common in the early days of the game. Other rule differences included tie games that went into sudden-death overtime (nowadays the shootout is applied), and no substitutes were allowed (if one player was injured and had to leave the ice, the other team also had to remove a player).

When the Canadian team finally arrived in Antwerp, they were surprised to see the conditions that they would be playing in. The dimensions of the natural-ice rink were considerably smaller than the Canadian standard, measuring approximately 50 metres long by 18 metres wide, whereas Canadian rinks are 61 metres long by 26 metres wide. The rinks in Antwerp had originally been constructed to accommodate the figure skaters and ice dancers, and not hockey players. The boards were assembled in panels, making for irregular bounces of the puck, and the Canadians actually questioned whether the boards would hold up in a game situation if a player was checked into them.

During the Games, organizers had installed netting around the entire rink to protect the paying customers. Organizers had also set up what can be called the historical precedent of luxury boxes. Chairs and tables were placed at one end of the rink for patrons who wanted to eat and drink while watching the action on the ice. As well as viewing the entertainment on the ice, fans also had the pleasure of listening to an orchestra that played ceaselessly from morning till night.

Among the other teams that showed up for the hockey competition—Czechoslovakia, Sweden, Belgium, Switzerland, France—only the United States had any real notion of how the game was actually played. Although the Canadians looked professional in their black and yellow uniforms, they were shocked to see the relative state of the other teams. One player on the French team sported a beard down to his chest and another was clearly well into his 40s. The Swedes showed up to the competition not with hockey sticks but with sticks from a traditional game called bandy. The Swedish version of bandy was played on ice; however, the arena was the size of a soccer field, and the Swedes used speed skates to enable them to get around faster. The speed skates were all well and good for playing bandy, but in hockey, the skates were of no benefit. The Swedes were excellent skaters when skating a straight line, but they could not match the stop-and-start agility of the Canadian players and were completely unprepared for the art of the body check. The Swedes also had no upper body padding, no shin guards and crude "hockey" gloves, and the goaltender was described as wearing "a cross between a blacksmith's apron and an aviator's coat."

Despite the unusual conditions they had to play under, the Canadian team got off to a great start.

With dreams of Olympic gold in their heads, the Canadian men's hockey team bulldozed their way through the competition, beating the U.S. (2–0), Sweden (12–1) and Czechoslovakia (15–0) by a combined score of 29–1. Along with receiving their shiny new medals, the Canadian hockey team was given an official piece of paper stating that they had won the hockey gold medal of the first official Winter Olympic Games.

The Winnipeg Falcons beamed with pride at the gold medals around their necks, knowing that they would go down in history as winning in the first-ever Winter Games. But years later the IOC repealed their decision to name the 1920 Olympic Games as the first Winter Games and handed that honour to the 1924 Chamonix, France, Winter Olympics.

At the 1924 Olympic Games, the Canadian hockey team again won the gold medal and was officially recognized as the first team to win Olympic hockey gold. It was not until many years later that the 1920

Winnipeg Falcons were recognized as official Olympic champions, though it was for the 1920 Summer Games!

1920 Olympic Hockey Team:
The Winnipeg Falcons

Goaltender	Wally Byron
Defense	Bobby Benson, Connie Johannesson
Centre	Frank Fredrickson (captain)
Forward	Chris Fridfinnson
Left Wing	Mike Goodman
Right Wing	Slim Halderson
Rover	Allan Woodman
Coach	Gordon Sigurjonson

The First Official Winter Hockey Gold: Chamonix, France

In June 1922, the French Olympic Committee invited athletes from around the world to participate in an international sports week that would feature hockey, skating and skiing events. Officially, the original title of the competition was the "Semaine internationale des sports d'hiver," but a year later, the IOC changed the name to the first official Winter Olympic Games.

With one ice hockey gold medal under its belt from the 1920 games, Canada sent an entirely new group of players to the 1924 Olympics in Chamonix, France, to show the world just how the game is played. The lucky team members to receive this honour were the Granite Club players from Toronto. The Canadians had little idea of the types of teams they would face in France, but they were prepared for anything as they had enough experience between them after playing against the tough teams of the southern Ontario leagues.

Hoping to get a firsthand account of the team's trip overseas, the *Toronto Telegram* daily newspaper hired left winger Harry Watson to report on his experiences at the Olympics. The intent was to save the paper some money at having to send their own reporter but also to give their readers a running social commentary on the international event. Watson, who turned out to be a decent writer, gave this account of the team's trip:

The trip started in a not too promising manner as the Bay of Fundy was on its bad behaviour and certainly showed its mean disposition with wind, rain and fog storm from the time we set sail till the morning of Jan. 12 (1924). The result was that most of us remained on deck till pretty late. Hooley Smith had bet me $1 that he wouldn't be seasick, but about 11 PM was counted out by referee P.J. Mulqueen. At this time Hooley's main cry was "And we've got to come back!" Breakfast was a very sad affair.

When they arrived in Chamonix, France, the Canadian team found that the conditions of the rink were no more favourable than what the team in 1920 had faced. Although the rink had a larger ice surface, the boards around the outdoor arena were only about one foot high. This put a dent in the Canadians' approach to the game, because using the boards for passing, and especially for hitting, was part of the way they played. Aside from the boards, an interesting fact is that large nets were placed behind the goals. Why did they put large nets behind the end boards? Well, the simple reason was that the rink was situated directly at the base of Mont Blanc, which was known to release an avalanche or two if disturbed. The nets would not stop the avalanche completely, but they might at least give people time to get away.

The weather was another factor that made the playing conditions less than perfect. The weather varied from extremes of warm sun to heavy rains, and the Granites were unable to get in one practice before playing their first game. To stay in game shape, the players were forced to workout off the ice by jogging and lifting weights. But despite the weather obstacles, which would have surely cancelled a game today, the team opened up the tournament with a series of decisive wins.

Looking back, the Granites were probably too seasoned for the level of competition that the international community threw at them given that the Canadians dominated the round-robin portion of the tournament, winning games against Czechoslovakia (30–0), Sweden (22–0) and Switzerland (33–0). It must have been almost comical to watch the swift-footed Canadians dance around the hapless international players. The Canadians controlled the puck for most of the games, so much so that goaltender Jack Cameron had a tough time maintaining an interest in the game and was frequently spotted skating over to the boards to chat up the young women in attendance.

By all accounts, the gold medal could have been handed off to the Canadians at that point, but they still had to finish out their remaining matches.

In the semifinal rounds, Canada was up against Great Britain. The Brits were tough opponents, but the Canadian squad still came out with a decisive 19–2 victory. The final, however, turned out to be more of a challenge. The United States had a much deeper history with the game of hockey than the other teams and was able to ice a higher quality team. But the challengers were still no match for the Granites, and the U.S. lost the final by a score of 6–1. Canada had its second straight Olympic hockey gold medal with no contenders in sight who could match their abilities. This first hockey gold medal established a long tradition of the game for Canadians in the Olympics.

1924 Olympic Hockey Team: The Toronto Granites

Goaltender	Jack Cameron, Ernie Collett
Defense	Dunc Munro (captain), Beattie Ransay
Centre	Hooley Smith
Left Wing	Cyril Slater, Harry Watson
Right Wing	Bert McCaffery, Harold McMunn
Coach	Frank Rankin

All Bow Before Mighty Canada!

After a thorough thrashing in the 1924 Olympics in France, the international hockey community was left licking its wounds by the time the 1928 Olympics in St. Moritz, Switzerland, rolled around. This time, the University of Toronto Grads represented Canada. The hockey team was one of the most talented in Canada at the time. They had won the Allan Cup the previous year and had the luxury of being coached by Conn Smythe, who had just become owner of the Toronto Maple Leafs in 1927.

The Grads were used to the pressure of crucial hockey games and had done battle with Canada's best teams. Many people had already anointed the Grads as gold medallists. This was exactly the reason that Olympic organizers decided to try something a little different for that year's tournament. Instead of the regular round-robin format followed by a series of playoffs, of the 10 teams that were registered for the event, nine were divided into three separate pools, and the winner of each pool went on to face the 10th team, which was Canada. The organizers wanted to ensure that each team to face Canada would be good enough at least to put up a respectable challenge.

But leading up to the start of the Games, Conn Smythe suddenly pulled out from his position as head coach of the Grads because of his increasing involvement with the NHL and handed off the job to W.A. Hewitt and his assistant coach, a wet-behind-the-ears Harold Ballard, the future much-maligned Toronto Maple Leafs owner. The Canadian team itself was looking forward to a challenge from the international community with the new changes; they simply did not want to be handed the title on a silver platter.

While the Canadians waited for the other teams to battle it out for the right to play in the final, left winger Dave Trottier was able to study the European's style of play and wrote an assessment of their skill level in his journal:

> *These European teams play a rough and ready game of close checking and that means that it will be hard to score against them if they can match our speed.*
>
> *Some of these players are exceptionally fine skaters, especially those from Switzerland and Norway, but their stickhandling and the finer points of hockey team play, fast snappy passing, pokechecking, dodging a man, drawing defense or goaler out—all these, instinctive in a Canadian player, are as yet an undeveloped art with the Europeans.... Our team should have no difficulty in beating anything I have seen but we are going to take no chances, and a game is never won until the final whistle blows.*

Up first was Sweden, which the Canadians promptly sent home with an 11–0 victory. Great Britain did not offer much of a resistance either, giving up the game by an even larger margin of 14–0. Despite the backing of their home crowd, the Swiss team was no challenge for the Canadian squad and went down by a final score of 13–0. (In case you weren't counting, that's 38 goals for Canada to zero!) For the third time in a row, Canada walked away with another Olympic gold medal in hockey.

After winning the gold, the Canadian team embarked on a whirlwind tour of Europe, stopping in Vienna, Berlin, Paris and London. Fans by the thousands came out to greet the Canadian Olympic champions and to see for themselves how the game was supposed to be played. After being feted all across Europe, the Canadian men returned home as champions.

1928 Olympic Hockey Team: University of Toronto Graduates

Goaltender	Norbert Mueller, Dr. Joe Sullivan
Defense	Frank Fisher, Roger Plaxton, John Porter (captain), Ross Taylor
Centre	Hugh Plaxton
Right Wing	Dr. Lou Hudson
Left Wing	Dave Trottier
Forward	Charlie Delahey, Grant Gordon, Bert Plaxton, Frank Sullivan
Coach	Conn Smythe

Finally, a Challenge:
Lake Placid, New York, 1932

Throughout Olympic hockey history, the United States has always been the proverbial thorn in the side for Canada, but as with all great rivalries, there has to be a starting point. In the three previous Olympics (1920, 1924 and 1928), Canada basically walked up unopposed and took the gold medal, but the 1932 Olympics in Lake Placid proved to be a turning point in Canada's dominance of the event.

For the first Winter Olympics on American soil, only four countries sent players to compete in the hockey event: Canada, the United States, Poland and Germany. Because of the relatively long distances that had to be travelled, fewer teams were able to attend the Winter Games in Lake Placid, New York. Canada sent as its representative the winners of the 1913 Allan Cup, the Winnipeg Hockey Club.

Prior to the start of the 1932 Olympics, the American team knew they would be in tough against the Canadians and tried anything to distract them from the upcoming games. Before arriving at Lake Placid for the Olympics, the Americans played an exhibition game against the Boston Bruins. Normally this would not have been an issue except that fans had to pay for the tickets, and the U.S. Olympic team pocketed a large portion of that money. Under amateur guidelines, this meant that the American hockey team had become professional.

The Canadian Olympic Committee (COC) responded by calling for the Americans to withdraw from the tournament, but the COC later relented, because if the Americans were removed, it would have left just three countries battling it out for gold.

The next problem arose when the Canadians were sent the schedule and discovered that they had to play nine games in 11 days. The Olympic organizers had pre-sold tickets to the hockey games based on eight countries participating, and when only four registered, the organizers did not want to refund the money. This meant that each of the four participating countries had to play two additional games. The Canadian contingent was furious over the schedule but again bent to the will of the American hosts.

With all the distractions before the start of the games, the Canadians were caught a little off guard by the Americans' skill on the ice. Because they were one of the best amateur teams in Canada, the Canadian hockey team was expected to win another gold medal, but in the first game of the round-robin tournament, Canada battled a tough American squad. Although Canada opened up the scoring in the second period, it was the only goal they could muster during regulation. The Americans tied it up in the third and held strong, pushing the game into overtime, a first for Canada at the Olympics. The overtime period solved absolutely nothing and another was required before Canada scored to win the game.

It was a sobering win for Canada, and as was soon revealed, the most important win of the Games.

Germany and Poland tried their best against Canada in the other round-robin games but were just not at the same level. In the four games Canada played against both countries, they outscored the other teams by a total of 28–1. The United States had nearly equal results against Poland and Germany and played Canada for the gold medal.

After regaining a little confidence playing against the weaker teams of Poland and Germany, Canada hoped to rebound strong in the final game against the U.S., but it didn't turn out that way. The U.S. continued to frustrate the Canadian forwards in their defensive zone and were a constant threat on attack. After three periods, both teams were once again tied and headed into overtime. The first overtime period went by and then the second, and still neither team gave up a goal. It was an epic battle, with more than a few sticks catching bare bone and a few broken egos. It was a fight for hockey supremacy, after all. Yet the game seemed to go on forever.

It was beginning to look as if everyone in the arena was going to have to stay up all night just to see the game through. After the end of the second overtime period, officials decided they had had enough. They ruled that the game be deemed a tie, and the gold medal would go to the team that won the earlier game in round-robin play. That team, of course, was Canada.

Although it was Canada's fourth straight hockey gold, it was a wake-up call to the nation's ego that other countries were quickly closing the ingenuity gap of hockey. It was a needed reminder that in order to remain at the top of the hockey world, Canada could not simply rest on its laurels. The best amateur team in Canada was no longer assured a gold medal. In order to maintain its stranglehold on the Olympics, Canada decided to create an all-star team of its own, selecting the best players from the amateur leagues, having them train together and then making a final cut before coming away with the best team to represent the country. This change in procedure was an important step in the evolution Canada's Olympic hockey program and was how future teams would be built.

1932 Olympic Hockey Team: The Winnipegs

Goaltender	William Cockburn (captain), Stanley Wagner
Defense	Roy Hinkel, Hugh Sutherland
Centre	George Garbutt, Walter Monson, Harold Simpson
Left Wing	Bert Duncanson, Romeo Rivers, Aliston Wise
Right Wing	Clifford Crowley, Victor Lindquist, Norm Malloy, Kenneth Moore
Coach	Jack Hughes

GOLD! Almost...

Under the watchful eye of Adolf Hitler and the National Socialist Party, the twin German towns of Garmisch-Partenkirchen played hosts to the fourth Winter Olympic Games in 1936. The Olympics are supposed to be about the nations of the world coming together in the spirit of friendship and understanding, and when Germany was awarded the Olympics in 1933, the world had not yet fully grasped the nature of what the country was to become.

IOC president Henri Baillet-Latour experienced a taste of Nazi hospitality when, on his way into the town of Garmisch, he saw a sign that read "Dogs and Jews Not Allowed." Baillet-Latour demanded that the sign be taken down at once, but Hitler replied that as a guest of the host nation, the IOC should accept and understand the host's culture. However, when the IOC president threatened to cancel the Olympics, Hitler capitulated and removed the sign.

At the opening ceremonies, 80,000 people filled the stadium, with nations from all over the world applauding their host Reichsführer Adolf Hitler as he officially opened the Games, completely unaware of the global horror their host would soon bring down on the world.

Going into the 1936 Games in Germany, Canada was still reeling from the sobering close call its hockey team had experienced at the 1932 Olympics and was not looking to this Olympics as a gimme. As was the tradition from earlier Olympics, Canada usually sent the winners of the Allan Cup, but 1936 was different. The Halifax Wolves, winners of the 1935 Allan Cup, were thought to be the team that would be heading overseas, but by the time the 1936 Games rolled around, many of the players had by then turned professional. Canadian hockey organizers were left without a team. It was then agreed that the runner-up of the Allan Cup, the Port Arthur Bear Cats, was best suited to take the Olympic challenge. The Bear Cats packed their bags and headed for European soil. However, this is where the story gets a little complicated.

At the very same time that the Bear Cats were crossing the Atlantic, another team of 14 amateur hockey players left Canada to play hockey in England as part of an exhibition tour. The players had failed to receive permission from the Canadian Amateur Hockey Association (CAHA) to play abroad and were thus suspended for their actions. The amateur players pleaded with the association to handle the case with lenience, and the CAHA capitulated. Two of the players were allowed to remain behind and play for Great Britain in the Olympics: goaltender James Foster and forward Alex Archer. With the addition of these two players to their roster, the British were starting to look as though they'd be a contending hockey team in the Olympics.

The Bear Cats got through the opening games of the hockey tournament in convincing fashion, beating Poland, Latvia and Austria. Canada's first opponent in the medal rounds turned out to be Great Britain. The CAHA soon regretted its decision to let the two Canadians, Foster and Archer, play for jolly ol' England.

In their game against the Brits, the Canadian attack was repelled wave after wave by goaltender James Foster. He had learned a few things during his years in the Canadian hockey system, and he was simply spectacular in the game versus Canada. Because of Foster's acrobatic efforts, Great Britain managed to squeak by with a 2–1 victory.

Canada brushed off the defeat with their heads still held high, knowing that they might get another chance against the Brits. The Bear Cats held to their game plan, dispatched their Czechoslovakian and U.S. challengers and were all set to play the Brits for the gold medal. But the final game never took place.

Olympic authorities suddenly changed the tournament format after the second round. Second-round matches now counted in the third-round standings, meaning that Canada's loss to Great Britain virtually eliminated them from the gold-medal round no matter how much they dominated the other teams.

Canadian Olympic official P.J. Mulqueen called it "one of the worst manipulations in sporting history." Canadian centre Hugh Farquharson added his thoughts to the controversy:

No one realized, and the officials at least should have, that to lose that first game meant probable loss of the title. It would have made a big difference if that were known when we went into our game with England. That pool system has been in use over there for many years. There is no excuse for not completely understanding it before a Canadian team left Canada.

The new rule stated that any team that had beaten another in a previous round did not have to play the same team in the finals. Thus, Great Britain's one win over Canada basically guaranteed that they couldn't play them for the gold. Canada's consolation prize was the silver medal, but it wasn't the medal they were expecting to leave with.

The Port Arthur Bear Cats were left with the historical stigma of being the team that ended Canada's four straight gold-medal reign by losing one early stage game by a single goal. Sometimes the hockey gods can be cruel deities, but Canada dusted itself off and returned looking for redemption in 1948, after the world returned to peace.

1936 Olympic Team:
Port Arthur Bear Cats

Goaltender	Francis Moore, Arthur Nash
Defense	Walter Kitchen, Ray Milton, Herman Murray (captain)
Centre	Hugh Farquharson, Alexander Sinclair
Left Wing	Maxwell Deacon, Ralph St. Germain
Right Wing	Dave Neville, Bill Thomson
Forward	Ken Farmer, Jim Haggarty
Coach	Al Pudas

The RCAF Flyers

Some 12 years after the 1936 Winter Olympics in Germany, Canada returned to the spirit of the Games looking to make their mark. The world had seen enough suffering and heartache because of World War II and was looking forward to putting the ugly past behind them.

The Olympic Committee did not have any trouble in choosing Switzerland as the host of the fifth Winter Olympic Games. Given the country's neutral stance during World War II, it was thought the perfect venue to welcome countries from around the world.

But as the world prepared for the 1948 Olympics, Canada was embroiled in a battle with the International Ice Hockey Federation (IIHF) for what it perceived as years of unfair rulings that were aimed specifically against the Canadians (that is, the 1936 controversy that lost Canada its medal to Great Britain). To protest the bias, the Canadian Amateur Hockey Association (CAHA) pulled its hockey team from the 1947 World Ice Hockey Championships.

As a result of this feud with the IIHF, just 100 days before the start of the 1948 Olympics in St. Moritz, Switzerland, Canada was still without a team to send over. Although some in the CAHA called for a boycott of the 1948 Olympics, the Royal Canadian Air Force (RCAF) volunteered their team to represent Canada.

At the time, the RCAF Flyers were the best team suited to represent Canada. Over the next few months, legendary NHL player Frank Boucher and his father George Boucher coached the RCAF team and set about preparing them with a series of exhibition games against minor league clubs. After poorly played games, some changes to the original lineup and George Boucher handing over the coaching position entirely to his son, the RCAF jumped on board the *Queen Elizabeth* in New York and headed across the Atlantic several weeks before the start of the Olympics.

Arriving in England on January 15, the Flyers embarked on a whirlwind tour of Europe, playing a series of exhibition games in Switzerland, Czechoslovakia, France, Belgium, Holland and Sweden, before finally setting off to St. Moritz for the start of the Olympics.

Because of the Canadians' late start in getting the team ready for the Olympics and the average showing in the exhibition games, Canada did not enter into the Games as the odds-on favourites to win the gold. The Czechoslovakian and Swiss teams were equally up to the contest, and the Canadian and American teams looked promising in their preliminary games as well. Added to the challenge was that all the games were played outdoors, which could hinder the Canadians' efforts and lend an air of unpredictability to the game.

Despite the negative atmosphere surrounding the Canadians' chances going into the tournament, Canada came out with a strong effort against the Swedes and a 3–1 victory. Having finally coalesced as a team, the Canadians won a string of games against Great Britain (3–0), Poland (15–0), Italy (21–1), the U.S. (12–3) and Austria (12–0).

The only team to give Canada trouble was Czechoslovakia. In the one game they played, neither team could score. Both goaltenders put on a show for the international spectators, playing to a 0–0 tie. With the final series of games set for February 8, Canada found itself tied with the Czechs in the standings, with each team having won six games and the one tie that they shared.

The rules stated that in case of a tie in the standings after the round robin, goal-average would be the deciding factor for the gold medal. The average was calculated by dividing the goals scored by the goals against. Before the final, Canada had scored 66 goals and only allowed five, which calculated out to a goal-average of 13.2. The Czechs, by comparison, scored 76 goals and allowed 15 goals, which calculated out to a goal-average of 5.0. All Canada had to do was win their final game against Switzerland and they would take home the gold medal, seeing as it was next to impossible for the Czechs to make up the goal-average differential. The Czechs would have had to score over 40 goals in their final game against the United States to have any hope of winning the gold.

Throughout the tournament, the Canadians had complained about the one-sided refereeing that was clearly in favour of the European teams. In the final game against the host Swiss team, the refereeing became a running joke for the Canadian players, as everything they did on the ice seemed to lead to a penalty. During the final two periods, when it was clear that the Canadians were in a far superior class than the Swiss and that the home team was about to lose, the crowd began to boo and throw snowballs at the Canadian players. But the boos, bad officiating and snowballs did little to stop Canada from winning the game 3–0, and when the final bell sounded, the Canadian players leaped onto the ice and posed for a picture at centre ice.

The RCAF trainer complained about the officiating after the game saying, "We played eight men—the Swiss players and the referees—and still beat 'em."

The 1948 Olympic Hockey Team: RCAF Flyers

Goaltender	Murray Dowey
Defense	Frank Dunster, Andre Laperriere, Louis Lecompte
Forward	Orval Gravelle, Patrick Guzzo, Wally Halder, Ted Hibberd, George Mara (captain), Ab Renaud, Reg Schroeter, Irving Taylor
Coach	Frank Boucher

How Sweet It Is!
1952 Olympics, Oslo, Norway

For the 1952 Winter Olympics, the Canadian Amateur Hockey Association (CAHA) chose the Edmonton Mercurys to represent Canada in Oslo, Norway, for the Games. The CAHA usually selected the winner of the Allan Cup, but the Western Senior League had moved into being semi-pro and was thereby disqualified from competition. The Mercurys were an intermediate senior A team that had an excellent history in international competition; having won the World Ice Hockey Championships in 1950, they were the perfect fit for the tournament.

To start their training for the Games, the Canadian team left for Europe in December 1951 to play in a series of exhibition games. This allowed them to get used to the European style of play and the larger ice surfaces. This was the first time that the Canadian hockey team travelled to the Games by plane, departing from Montréal to land in Scotland. One hour after landing, the Mercurys were on the ice playing against the Scottish Ayr Raiders. The Mercurys started off with a 6–3 victory and continued their barnstorming tour through England and then on into European mainland.

Everywhere they went, the Mercurys gave the European hockey fans a show they would never forget. Many of them had never before seen players with such speed and strength coupled with a team unity that made their play on the ice seamless. The tour, however, was put on hold when an incident occurred as the team was making its way from one game to another.

The entire team was packed in a bus heading for an exhibition game against a Norwegian team at the stadium in Oslo where all the Olympic games would be played. As the bus was rounding a curve on the road to Oslo, one of the wheels locked and the bus careened off the road, jumped over a ditch and toppled against a tree. Luckily the accident was a minor one, and only three players suffered slight injuries. Taking one day to shake off the scare, the players were back on the ice and beat the Norwegians 7–2 before a crowd of 10,000 fans.

As much as the European fans enjoyed the Canadian brand of hockey, many in the European media disliked the physical side to Canada's game. Ever since hockey was added as an Olympic sport in 1920, the IOC had been playing by the "Canadian" rules of the game, and there had always been disagreements as to the interpretation of the checking rule. European newspapers characterized the Canadian game as goonish and stated that the physical aspect of the game was taken to a level where it was used simply as a tool of intimidation. The Canadians, however, were not about to change their style for a few critics.

In the Mercurys' first three games of the tournament, they showed the world that they had come to play and did not care one bit about the objections to their style of hockey. They trounced the Germans (15–1), the Finns (13–3) and the Poles (11–0) by a combined score of 39–4. The Czechs provided the first challenge to the Canadian squad, but Canada still ended up winning the game 4–1.

The Swedes, however, were a different story. It was apparent in the first period of the game against Canada that the Europeans had come a long way since the first Olympic tournament in 1920. The Swedes' passing was tape to tape, and they were not afraid of getting physical in the corners. After just 10 minutes of play, the Swedes put two goals by Canadian goaltender Ralph Hansch on four shots in the entire period. Canadian hockey was suddenly faced with the prospect that it might not be the best in the world.

Luckily, Canadian forward Louis Secco scored, bringing the Canadians within one before the end of the first period. In the second, Canada turned up the pace of the game, but Swedish goaltender Thord Flodquist kept deflecting shot after shot to keep his team in the game. However, before the period was out, the Canadians managed to tie the score on a goal by forward George Abel. The third period saw more of the same acrobatics by Flodquist, but Canadian captain

Billy Dawe managed to score the game winner with just 20 seconds left in the final period.

The Mercurys happily took the win but with the realization that the gold medal was no longer a sure thing. CAHA president Doug Grimston was quick to note the change in the level of competition, saying, "European teams have improved considerably the last few years and, with some proper coaching, could be mighty troublesome to Canada."

Canada followed up the win over the Swedes with a self-affirming 11–2 trouncing of Norway. The Mercurys' final game of the tournament was played against the United States. Because the U.S. had already lost a game to the Swedes, the Canadians were assured the gold medal. The Americans played the same tight, defensive, physical hockey as the Canadians and battled them to a 3–3 tie. Canada walked away with the gold medal yet again. As they celebrated their hard-earned victory, little did they know that it would be 50 years before Canada would again be named the best team in the world.

Between 1920 and 1952, Canadian hockey teams compiled an outstanding record of 37 wins, one loss and three ties. In the 41 games that they played, Canada scored a total of 403 goals while only allowing their opponents to score 34. But as Doug Grimston had predicted, things were about to change.

1952 Olympic Hockey Team:
Edmonton Mercurys

Goaltender	Ralph Hansch, Eric Patterson
Defense	John Davies, Don Gauf, Bob Meyers, Tom Pollock, Al Purvis
Forward	George Abel, Billy Dawe (captain), Bruce Dickson, Billy Gibson, David Miller, Gordie Robertson, Louis Secco, Frank Sullivan, Robert Watt
Coach	Lou Holmes

The Losing Years: 1956 to 1998

At the 1956 Olympics in Cortina d'Ampezzo, Italy, Canada experienced a harsh lesson, one that it knew was a long time coming; the hockey world had finally caught up to it. At the top of the list of the new skilled countries were the U.S. and the USSR. Both countries had thrown a significant amount of money into their hockey programs in the interval leading to the Olympics, and it was finally starting to pay dividends. Although many of the European teams still saw the Canadians as the favourites to repeat their gold-medal performance, Canada knew that this would be their toughest Winter Games to date.

The Canadian team, represented by the Kitchener-Waterloo Dutchmen, was for the first time praised by the international media for their fair play and sportsmanship. Since 1920, Canada had been vilified for their "overly" physical style of play; however, at the 1956 Games, that stigma was put upon the American and Soviet teams. Despite the rise of new challengers to Canadian supremacy, the team was feeling confident of its chances.

The preliminary round started out as the Canadian team had planned, winning all three of their games by a combined score of 30–1. But the true test came in their opening medal-round game against the Americans. In goal for Canada was Denis Brodeur (father of New Jersey Devils netminder Martin Brodeur), and he would face Canada's greatest test in Olympic history. In the preliminary rounds, the Americans had lost to the Czechs and barely squeaked by Poland to make it into the medal rounds, but as history tells, the U.S. players always pick up their play in games against Canada.

In the first period, it was clear to the Canadian bench that the Americans had come to play. Within the first two minutes, the U.S. put the opening goal behind Brodeur and were constantly on the attack. At 9:23 of the first, the Americans took a 2–0 lead that sent the Canadians into panic mode. In the second period, Canada peppered American goaltender Willard Ikola with 16 shots but managed to get only one in the net. That was the best the Canadian squad could do. The U.S. potted two more on their way to a 4–1 upset.

The loss effectively removed Canada from contending for the gold medal and sent an entire country into mourning. CBC Radio broadcaster Thom Benson had a solemn and dramatic view of what the loss meant to Canadian hockey. The following is an excerpt taken from his broadcast on February 1, 1956:

Today, in this small mountain village, there was a funeral. The bells of the ancient church told the passing of a procession. The mourners chanted prayers as they trudged up the steep hills behind the coffin bearers. Those who were left were saying their farewells to a robust and lively friend.

The cortege wound its through narrow and twisted streets up past the Concordia Hotel. Inside that building, there was a similar ceremony where the inhabitants mourned the passing of an era. In the hotel was housed the Kitchener-Waterloo hockey team and all those other Canadians who aspired to Olympic heights in the field of amateur competition.

There was no joy there, no happy words, no jubilation, for last night Canadian amateur hockey suffered a blow to its prestige from which it may never recover. The Kitchener-Waterloo team was beaten fairly and squarely by a team, which would never make the junior finals in Canada. If you think saying that is easy, then you are greatly mistaken.

While the Canadian team was left licking its wounds, the USSR was quietly winning all its games. If Canada had any hope of winning the gold, it had to beat the Soviets to tie its record and score a handful of goals to beat them in the goal-average tiebreaker. The U.S. had lost its game against the Soviets, so the Canadians had some hope for the gold. But the Soviets were not in a giving mood and shutout Canada in the final game 2–0. This left the team with a 3–2 record and a third-place finish, good enough for the bronze. In 36 years of Olympic hockey, this was Canada's worst-ever performance and signalled the dawn of a new era in international ice hockey competition. It was becoming evident by the minute that to continue to compete, Canada was going to have to change the way it operated in amateur hockey. However, it was also clear that the Soviets were not being altogether honest in their definition of the word "amateur."

On the other side of the Iron Curtain, the Soviets ran a program that trained their players for eight to 10 months out of the year, playing in their "amateur" leagues. The Soviets denied vehemently that their players were of professional calibre, but other countries knew quite clearly what was going on. It was an issue that would dominate the next several Olympics.

The 1960 Winter Olympics in Squaw Valley saw a change for all future players who represented Canada. While the Kitchner-Waterloo Dutchmen returned to the Games and played up to their potential, it was clear the rest of the world was not sticking to the rules that defined who exactly was an amateur. The Soviets were obviously not playing by the rules, and the amateur status of other countries was questionable. Canada played a solid tournament but again lost a game to the Americans in the medal round and were knocked out of gold-medal contention.

For the next Olympics, the CAHA decided it was time to change the way things operated. A year before the start of the 1964 Olympics in Innsbruck, Austria, the CAHA agreed that the team to represent Canada should be selected from the best amateurs in university and senior A as early as possible. Forming the team early would allow the players the time to get accustomed to playing together. Some wondered whether the new system would work, but the previous two Olympics had proven that the old ways no longer worked.

The first edition of Team Canada won the opening game of the tournament 14-1 over a hopelessly outplayed Yugoslavian team. In the medal round, Canada faired well in their first four games, but the greatest test came against a tough Czech team and a final match against the Soviets. Canada played hard in the opening game against the Czechs, taking a 1–0 lead into the third period. Canada's goaltender Seth Martin was having an outstanding game, but with less than 10 minutes left in the final period, he collided with a Czech player in front of his goal and had to be taken out of the match.

Backup goaltender Ken Broderick hadn't played all tournament long and looked rusty from his opening save. In the final seven minutes of the game, the Czechs put three goals by Broderick for a final 3–1 victory. The Canadian squad was devastated, and although they tried their best in the final game against the Soviets, the loss of Martin was too much to bounce back from, and they finished out the Olympics in fourth place.

The 1968 Olympics in Grenoble, France, was no different for Team Canada as the Soviets once again were the clear favourites to win gold. The Canadians put together a series of good games, but two losses to Finland and the Soviets gave them the bronze medal. After a run of disappointing international results, Canada was left wondering how to start winning hockey games again. The problem became so bad that in the 1968 federal election, Prime Minister Pierre

Trudeau promised to commission a special task force on sports, with the aim of understanding the gap between Canadian and international hockey. The result was the formation of Hockey Canada in February 1969. Its first order of business was an attempt at evening the playing field with the other "amateurs" of the world.

As Canada was set to host the World Championships in 1970, it seemed like the perfect moment to press the IIHF for changes to international competition. Hockey Canada's goal was to make the competition open to professionals so that the competition would be a truer reflection of the country's level of talent. The IIHF agreed to allow each team to have nine non-NHL pros in each international tournament for one year just to see how things evolved.

When the first tournament came along, Canada used only five pros and finished a close second to the Soviets. Just a few days later, the IIHF held an emergency meeting and completely reversed their decision, saying that any player competing with Canada's pros would be forfeiting their amateur status and would therefore be ineligible to play in the Olympics. This sudden change of heart infuriated Hockey Canada, and in a bold move, they withdrew Team Canada from all future international competitions, including the Olympics. The protest made it clear to the world that Canada would not continue to compete in international tournaments and abide by the rules while the rest of the world basically cheated. Hockey Canada held firm and missed out on the 1972 Olympics in Sapporo, Japan, and the 1976 Olympics in Innsbruck, Austria (both gold medals were won by the "amateur" Soviets).

When Canada returned to the Olympics in 1980, things got much worse for the men in red and white. At Lake Placid, New York, Canada settled for sixth place; at the 1984 Games in Sarajevo they took fourth; on home turf in Calgary in 1988 they again finished a disappointing fourth, despite having a few professional players in the roster; and finally at the 1992 Games in Albertville, France, things turned around, and they finished with a silver medal. The 17th Winter Games in Lillehammer, Norway, in 1994 again brought a silver medal, but in Canada, it was gold that mattered.

Canada finally saw a ray of hope of breaking the European hold on gold when it was announced before the start of the 1998 Nagano Games that the NHL would suspend its season to allow the best NHL players to represent their countries.

The Winter Olympics in Nagano, Japan, however, proved to be a disaster for Canada's best hopes. Not even the great Wayne Gretzky could help the team to the gold medal. In fact, they had to settle for fourth place. Hope for Canadian hockey was at an all-time low. But in 2002, Canada returned with a lineup of players hoping to make history.

2002 Olympic Return

After the heartbreaking loss to the Czech Republic at the 1998 Nagano Olympics, Canadian hockey fans looked to the 2002 Salt Lake City Olympics as the place for Canada to take the gold medal. As in the 1998 Olympics, the pressure for national glory once again fell on Canada's superstar ambassador of hockey, Wayne Gretzky, who this time led the team not as a player but as team general manager.

The doubters, deniers and unbelievers were at the ready to watch the Canadians be denied the Olympic gold again. None felt the pressure more than the players selected for the task of bringing the title back to Canada. Led by team captain Mario Lemieux, the Canadian squad included Joe Sakic, Jarome Iginla, Paul Kariya, Steve Yzerman, Chris Pronger, Theoren Fleury, Al MacInnis and stellar goaltender Martin Brodeur. The Canadian squad was one of the top teams, though it was the Czechs and the Russians who were pre-tournament favourites.

"We all know the pressure we have here in the next 10 days," said Mario Lemieux in a Canadian Press interview. "We're all professionals here, we all know what's at stake, we have a lot of confidence in each other and I think it's going to show over the next 10 days."

However, the tournament did not start out the way many were hoping, as the Canadians looked a little off in their first few games. They were beaten by the better-prepared Swedes 5–2 in the first game and seemed unsteady in their 3–2 victory over perennial losers Germany. Coach Pat Quinn seemed unsure of his lineups, and the players did not look as though they had had enough time to practice together to get a feel for each other's style. Critics quickly jumped on the shaky Canadian start, saying that the team wasn't good enough and that the rookie talent Gretzky had placed on the team could not stand the pressure of an international event such as the Olympics. The pressure came to a head when Canada played to a 3–3 tie with the Czech Republic. The international and Canadian media blasted the team for not playing up to the capabilities that its roster showed and for once again proving that Canada did not have what it took to win on the international stage. Players from other teams chimed in, trying to knock the team off their game.

Czech winger Martin Rucinsky openly criticized the Canadian team after the game: "We don't care about Canada. We don't take them as the team to beat. I don't think they're even close to being the best team in the tournament. You've seen that by the scores."

Gretzky had seen and heard enough. Not known for losing his temper, the Great One lashed out at the media and those who said his team would not make it far in the tournament.

"No one wants us to win except the guys on this team and our fans, but we're a proud team and we're still standing," said Gretzky after the game with the Czechs. "It turns my stomach to hear some of the things being said about us. To a man, every one of our guys will say how great (Dominik) Hasek or (Mats) Sundin is. I don't think we dislike the other countries nearly as much as they hate us."

Gretzky took a lot of flack for his comments, but it seemed to light a fire under the Canadian players, who easily beat Belarus 7–1 in their next game and moved on to the gold-medal game versus the Olympic host, the United States.

Fifty years to the day, Canada was set to play the same country they had played when it last won Olympic gold. For Canadians across the country, the game meant more than a gold in the Olympics—it was reward for 50 years of living in the shadow of countries that did not have the history and passion for hockey that Canada has for the game. In those dry years, nobody remembered who came in second.

The Americans were not an easy team for the Canadians to beat. The U.S. team had improved their play as the tournament progressed and had a generous amount of confidence after achieving a hard-fought victory against the ferocious Russian squad. The Americans had the prolific scoring talents of players Brett Hull, Mike Modano, Tony Amonte, Doug Weight and the solid-under-pressure goaltending of Mike Richter.

Even politicians turned out to view the game. Deputy Prime Minister John Manley represented Canada, while the U.S. brought out Vice President Dick Cheney to watch the two neighbouring countries do battle on the ice.

After the boring opening game ceremony, the crowd livened up as the teams circled in their own zone, ready to take the first faceoff of the game. Although U.S. fans were clearly in the majority, the Canadian contingent was conspicuous with Team Canada jerseys and Canadian flags dotting the arena.

The U.S. came out of the gate first, springing several two-on-one breaks into the Canadian zone. They got a goal by forward Tony Amonte at 8:49 of the first period when goaltender Martin Brodeur was caught off guard. This was the first time in the tournament that the Americans had been the first to score, but the Canadian team did not crumble.

They got their confidence back on one of the prettiest goals of the tournament. Controlling the puck through the neutral zone, defenseman Chris Pronger, with Mario Lemieux and Paul Kariya, moved into the U.S. defensive zone where two U.S. defensemen waited. The Mario Lemieux of the late 1980s returned for a brief moment of magic when he avoided the Pronger pass by letting it glide through his legs, faking out the two defensemen and the goaltender who thought that Lemieux was going to take the shot. Instead, Lemieux let the puck go to Kariya, who scored with an easy snap-shot into the open net. This highlight-reel goal energized Team Canada, who, led by Joe Sakic, took control of the game from then on.

Sakic was the all-around best player with the perfect mix of defensive strategy and offensive intelligence. He set up Jarome Iginla with a goalmouth pass that put Canada up 2–1 going into the second period. Brian Rafalski on the U.S. team tied the game on a power-play goal with less than five minutes remaining in the second period and brought the quiet American fans back to life. But the celebrations stopped short when Sakic put Canada back on top with a power-play goal of his own with just 1:20 remaining in the period. Canada went into the dressing room for the second intermission confident that they could put the game away in the third.

The third period was the most intense of the match as the Americans sought to get a crucial goal or two. The Canadians held firm, and Martin Brodeur kept his team alive with spectacular saves. The crowd noise swelled to a deafening roar that made the 8250 fans seem more like 18,000. Every person in the arena was on the edge of his or her seat, including Canadian team manager Wayne Gretzky who jumped and gasped like every other Canadian fan in the building and at home watching the game.

Worries of a U.S. comeback were wiped aside with Canada's fourth goal. Steve Yzerman, who had just returned to the ice after serving two tense minutes in the penalty box for tripping, passed the puck to Iginla. Iginla blasted a shot at the top corner that Richter stopped with his glove, but the puck fell to the ice and rolled over the goal line to put Canada up 4–2 with four minutes remaining in the third period.

Joe Sakic sealed the deal just two minutes later with a breakaway goal. As the buzzer sounded the end of the game, Martin Brodeur leapt into the air and was quickly surrounded by his teammates. Fifty years to the day, Canada was once again at the top.

"We had a great game plan in place and played it to a T," said Chris Pronger in a Canadian Press interview after the game. "And Marty Brodeur made some great stops towards the end to preserve the victory."

The significance of the win could be seen on the face of each player as the gold medal was placed around his neck. As the Canadian anthem played, many had tears of joy in their eyes for what they had just accomplished.

"It's unbelievable," said Pronger. "It's something you'll always be able to cherish, especially having it here in North America."

Hockey fans across Canada celebrated the gold-medal win, knowing that there wasn't an easy road to victory, which made winning the gold even sweeter. Next stop, Olympic Winter Games 2006?

2002 Canadian Olympic Hockey Team

Goaltender	Ed Belfour, Martin Brodeur, Curtis Joseph
Defense	Rob Blake, Eric Brewer, Adam Foote, Ed Jovanovski, Al MacInnis, Scott Niedermayer, Chris Pronger
Forward	Theo Fleury, Simon Gagne, Jarome Iginla, Paul Kariya, Mario Lemieux (captain), Eric Lindros, Joe Nieuwendyk, Owen Nolan, Mike Peca, Joe Sakic, Brendan Shanahan, Ryan Smyth, Steve Yzerman
Head Coach	Pat Quinn

Canadian Women Just Keep on Winning

At the same time that Canada watched its men's team win gold at the Salt Lake City 2002 Winter Olympic Games, another Canadian hockey team made Olympic history of its own.

In the early 1990s, Canadian women's hockey existed in the shadow of the more popular and better-funded men's national hockey program. The first international women's hockey tournament was barely mentioned in the media, and the women's neon pink uniforms did not help in promoting this new venture in sport. Even though Canadian women won the first World Championship in 1990, winning all five of their games and scoring 61 goals, it was the men's team that got all the attention.

Regardless of the lack of attention they were getting, the Canadian women's team dominated the international scene, winning the World Championship again in 1992, 1994 and 1997. After the '97 championship win, the public started to come around, and the media jumped on the rivalry that was developing between the Canadians and the Americans. At the beginning of 1997, the U.S. women's team could not match the skill of Canada, but over the year they worked hard to develop a solid core group of players, led by Cammi Granato, who were eventually able to challenge the Canadian team and provide some exciting hockey for fans.

That was the situation as women's hockey prepared to play for the first time in the 1998 Winter Olympics in Nagano, Japan. Now that national pride was on the table, Canadian women hockey players were provided with special training regimens, coaches and all the perks that the men's teams had long enjoyed.

Canada and the U.S. easily made their way through the other countries at the 1998 Olympics and found themselves again facing each other in the gold-medal game. The United States wanted revenge for their razor-thin defeat at the 1997 World Championships, which they had lost in overtime on a goal from Canadian Nancy Drolet.

The Canadian team had everything to lose in this game. They had held the title of World Champions since international women's hockey first began. The team wanted to prove in the inaugural Olympic women's hockey game that they were the best.

Unfortunately, Canada didn't play like the team that had won all the earlier tournaments. The gold-medal game began with the United States taking control immediately, connecting most of their passes and getting a flurry of shots off at overworked Canadian goaltender Manon Rheaume. Canada played like a team of individuals and not the effective unit they had once been. In the final minutes of the third period, the U.S. was leading 2–1. Canada pulled their goaltender for an extra attacker, hoping to tie the game and send it into the overtime period. But the Canadians could not keep control of the puck, and the Americans scored an empty-net goal for a 3–1 victory, winning the first gold medal for Olympic women's hockey. The emotion of the moment overcame the Canadian team, who felt the hopes of their country on their shoulders.

"At first, you feel disbelief," said Canadian team captain Stacy Wilson after the loss. "You have a dream for so many years and all of a sudden it's over. Then, the thoughts go through your head of your family and friends all over Canada…and thoughts lead to feelings. You see the medal and its silver-feelings kick in pretty quick."

"They were extremely hungry," Canadian defender Judy Diduck said of the U.S. team. "We've been on top so long, we won all the major tournaments. They were determined to knock us off."

Canada regained some confidence with a World Championship win in 1999 and was ready to meet the United States for a rematch at the 2002 Winter Olympic Games in Salt Lake City. The Canadian team went in as the favourites to win the silver and were not expected to provide a challenge to the U.S. team that had won eight games in a row against the Canadian squad during the season leading up to the Olympics.

Assistant captain and arguably the heart of the Canadian team, Hayley Wickenheiser said before the tournament started, "I've never lost eight games in a row in my entire hockey career. This is tough but it's going to make Salt Lake City that much better. We have a lot to prove, and we have nothing to lose now."

The Canadian squad played their system in the first few games and dominated the competition, beating Kazakhstan 7–0, Russia 7–0 and Sweden 11–0. Canadian goaltender Kim St. Pierre made the key saves while her teammates ran away with the game. Canada was on a high. Canadian jerseys popped up all over the arena as the tournament went on, and the chants of "Go, Canada, Go!" got louder and louder.

The first real challenge of the tournament for the Canadian women came when they faced off against a much-improved Finnish team. The game went according to plan for the Canadians in the first period, with the team potting the first two goals and ending the period ahead 2–1 after a late Finland goal.

Canada made 22 shots on the Finnish goal in the second period but could not get the puck behind tiny Finnish goaltender Tuula Puputti. By the end of the second period, Finland had scored two more goals and were poised to upset Canada.

Despite the sobering score, the Canadian players did not change their game plan when the third period got underway. Their continuing hard offense eventually paid off. The Finnish goaltender did her best to keep the Canadians at bay but could not stop all the shots.

Three minutes into the third period, Hayley Wickenheiser and Jayna Hefford scored two nice breakaway goals just six seconds apart. After that, the Finnish team could not hold the Canadians. Canada ended the game with a 7–3 victory and a path to the gold-medal game against their rivals, the United States. Canada went into the final game feeling confident they could win.

"Our team is good enough to win gold," said Canadian defenseman Geraldine Heaney in a Canadian Press interview after the game against Finland. "We came here for a gold medal and nothing else. It comes down to one game and anything can happen."

The Americans were the odds-on favourites, having been undefeated in their previous 35 games. The hometown U.S. crowd welcomed their team with a roof-raising cheer as the teams hit the ice for the pre-game skate. Canadian fans supporting their country's team were a sea of red and white. Wayne Gretzky showed up with a large contingent from the Canadian men's squad to cheer on their female counterparts. The noise of the crowd was deafening as the American referee dropped the puck to start the gold-medal game.

The Americans seemed nervous in the first few minutes of the game, and the Canadians quickly capitalized with a goal by left winger Caroline Ouellette at just 1:45 in the first period. As the period came to a close, Canada knew that they had the Americans scrambling. The Canadian team was controlling the flow of the game despite four questionable penalties given to Canada by American referee Stacey Livingston.

More penalties against Canada came at the start of the second period, and the Americans overcame the goaltending of Kim St. Pierre on a power-play goal by Katie King. Just a few minutes later, Canada restored its lead with a goal by Wickenheiser. The Canadians were winning the battle on the ice and also in the stands, as fans screamed, "Go, Canada, Go!"

The chant grew louder after a dramatic goal from Canada's Jayna Hefford in the final seconds of the second period. After a breakdown in the neutral zone by the American defence, Hefford had picked up a loose puck and outskated a defenseman for a breakaway on U.S. goaltender Sara DeCosta. As Hefford broke in over the American blue line, with the defenseman on her tail, she fumbled with the puck but somehow managed to poke it over the sprawled-out goaltender with one second remaining on the clock. It wasn't the prettiest of breakaway goals, but Canada now had a two-goal cushion going into the third period.

The U.S. managed to get within one goal, but they couldn't overcome the goaltending of St. Pierre. As the seconds peeled off the clock, the Canadians were confident they would be wearing Olympic gold around their necks this time.

"We stayed calm. We could see the fear in their eyes," said Wickenheiser after the game.

In the dying seconds of the game, the Canadian national anthem could be heard throughout the arena in a show of support for the team that no one expected would beat the Americans. When the clock ran out, the Canadian bench cleared, and the team surrounded their star goaltender in celebration.

This time it was the Canadians' turn to stand proudly with the gold medals around their necks and to listen to their anthem. They had earned the victory. They had earned their moment in the spotlight.

2002 Women's Olympic Hockey Team

Goaltender	Kim St. Pierre, Sami Jo Small
Defense	Thérèse Brisson, Isabelle Chartrand, Geraldine Heaney, Becky Kellar, Cheryl Pounder, Colleen Sostorics
Forward	Dana Antal, Kelly Bechard, Jennifer Botterill, Cassie Campbell (captain), Lori Dupuis, Danielle Goyette, Jayna Hefford, Caroline Ouellette, Cherie Piper, Tammy Lee Shewchuk, Vicky Sunohara, Hayley Wickenheiser
Coach	Danièle Sauvageau

Hayley Wickenheiser

In a CBC interview in 1994, 15-year-old Hayley Wickenheiser talked about her talents as a hockey player, the "female Wayne Gretzky" comparisons and the possibility of one day playing in a men's professional hockey league. Hayley responded aptly to the reporter's questions, saying, "I guess I would want to do that, but I don't know if it would be realistic. The size and the strength differences are so incredible that it's pretty tough to do."

At 15, Hayley was too young and too small to be playing against men in a full contact game. She needed to refine certain aspects of her game to be able to play on a competitive level with a men's team. The Women's National Team provided the perfect training ground for the young hockey star to sharpen her talents. At her young age she was already a member of the Women's World Championship team, and as each year went by, Hayley's skills as a hockey player improved. But the obvious physical difference between men and women would be something that she could never overcome.

"I will never be able to play like the guys do. So I just had to rethink my game," Hayley said. "I prefer to use brains over brawn."

The strategy worked for Wickenheiser. She continued to put up impressive numbers on the Women's National Team and was always considered a dominant figure on the ice, never afraid to lead with her body. The peak of her career with the Women's National Team came when Wickenheiser and her teammates dethroned the Americans to take the gold medal at the 2002 Winter Olympics in Salt Lake City.

"I looked at the Olympic gold in my hand and knew that I had gone as far as I could in women's hockey. The only place left where I still had something to prove to myself and to people around me was in a men's professional league."

Hayley wasted no time in vaulting the next hurdle. She went on to conquer men's professional hockey in Europe, playing in a Finnish men's league. In 2003 she scored her first point, setting a new standard for women's hockey. Going into the 2010 Olympics, she looks to lead the Canadian women to a new level and back to the title of World Olympic Champs.

The Lucky Loonie Story

How does a Zamboni driver from Edmonton, Alberta, become a legend of Canadian hockey? Simply by giving up a dollar.

At the 2002 Olympics in Salt Lake City, Utah, Olympics officials wanted to provide the hockey tournament with the best ice possible. There were local people they could choose from to be the ice caretaker, but the officials wanted the finest. Olympic hockey coordinator Nate Anderson sent a letter to a Mr. Trent Evans, ice technician for the Skyreach Centre, home of the Edmonton Oilers, and offered him the job of overseeing the ice preparation and maintenance during the Olympics. This was no random selection. The officials behind the decision had consulted sources in the NHL and every one of them had recommended Evans for the job. After all, every player in the NHL knows that the Oilers have the best ice in the league, so why not recruit the best for the Games?

It was the opportunity of a lifetime for Evans—to bring Canadian ice to the Olympics when Canada's men had a chance to bring gold back home after a 50-year absence. He accepted the offer and got ready to fly out to Salt Lake City, but before getting on the plane, he made sure to stop at a local Tim Hortons to buy a coffee. He handed the cashier a five-dollar bill, and she handed him back his change. He didn't think twice about the coins jingling in his pocket, but one coin in particular would soon change his life.

The date on the loonie that Evans put in his pocket was 1987. It was a big year for Canada in international hockey. In September 1987, the Canada Cup tournament, held in Hamilton and Montréal, came down to a final between the Soviet Red Army and Team Canada. The Canadians were led by a Wayne Gretzky at the peak of his career and by a young superstar named Mario Lemieux. In the best-of-three Cup final, the Soviets won the first game 6–5, but Canada bounced back with a win in game two. And in game three, Gretzky set up Lemieux for the game- and Cup-winning goal. To this day, it is hailed as the second greatest goal in Canadian hockey history (second only to Paul Henderson's goal in the 1972 Summit Series). Since that fateful game in 1987, Mario Lemieux had not played another game for the national team. Fifteen years later, Wayne Gretzky, acting as direction general manager for the 2002 Olympic team, selected Mario Lemieux as Canada's captain.

Trent Evans could not have pocketed a more poignant loonie that day at Tim Hortons. When he arrived at Salt Lake City, Evans noticed that the ice rink at the arena did not have a centre faceoff circle. To make sure he had the correct measurements, he fished in his pocket and pulled out that loonie. It was the perfect marker. He placed the loonie at centre ice when no one was looking and began flooding the ice so that the coin sat just a fraction of an inch below the surface. After the water froze over, Trent was the only person who knew of the loonie's existence in the ice—as long as he didn't tell anyone, of course. But he realized that such a story might help the Canadian players and the country get behind the team, so he began to tell others of the loonie.

But the story of the loonie below the ice spread quickly, and when Olympic officials got wind that a Canadian ice technician had done something to the ice, Evans was ordered to remove the loonie. The problem was that no one supervised the coin's removal, and Evans simply left the coin in its place. This time he kept the secret and told only those who needed to know: Team Canada, both the men's and the women's side.

"I'll give you the loonie if I can get it out after the big game," Trent said to Wayne before the Games got underway.

"We'll be tripping over each other trying to get at it," Wayne replied.

As the Games began, the lucky loonie under the ice seemed to work its magic. The Canadian women's hockey team made it into the final game against their hated rivals, the Americans, and managed to win the game and the gold medal. When the final bell sounded, the Canadian bench cleared, and the women tossed their equipment up in the air in celebration. Coming out to clear off the ice for the medal ceremony was

Trent Evans, and as he was pushing the helmets and gloves out of the way, he saw something that almost gave him a heart attack. Three of the Canadian players were pointing down at the ice where the loonie was buried. Hayley Wickenheiser also noticed the players at centre and raced over to them.

"I went and kissed centre ice," said Canadian forward Danielle Goyette. "Hayley came over and said to me, 'Get away, Danielle. We can't tell people it's there. The men's final is in three days, and we have to keep it secret.'"

But the secret held, and the loonie was in place for the men's final, Canada versus the United States. Millions of Canadians tuned in to watch the game billed as one of the greatest since the 1972 Summit Series. During the warm-up, Canadian players could be seen gently tapping the spot at centre ice for good luck. Trent Evans' little loonie had taken on a life of its own. Canada went on to beat the Americans 5–2, winning the country's first Olympic gold medal in 50 years.

After the game, Evans went into the Canadian dressing room and presented the coin to Gretzky. Gretzky didn't want to keep it; he just wanted to borrow it. Moments later, before a packed media room, Gretzky pulled out the loonie from his pocket and preceded to tell the world the story of the icemaker from Edmonton and the lucky coin. When Gretzky said the word "loonie," the world media was left scratching their heads. He had to spell it out for them. "L-o-o-n-i-e. Like the bird. It was for good luck. So I guess it worked."

After the press conference, Gretzky returned the coin to Evans and said, "You're going to be a legend."

The loonie ended up in the Hockey Hall of Fame, a place where all Canadians could see the coin and get a taste of the precious good luck charm.

Asked what he would have done with the coin if both the men's and women's teams had not won gold, Evans replied, "Simple. Dug it out and taken it home—and probably used it the next morning to buy a coffee on the way into work."

The 2010 Canadian Hope

With the 2010 Winter Olympic Games in Vancouver fast approaching, there is no shortage of talent available for executive director of Team Canada Steve Yzerman to choose from as he looks ahead at the task of assembling the men's Olympic hockey team. There will also be no shortage of pressure for Team Canada to perform before a crowd with extremely high expectations. The job might seem easy when looking at the short list of players available—and as the 2006 Winter Olympics showed, Canada might have selected the best team to win, but it doesn't always translate into success on the ice.

Pat Quinn, head coach of Team Canada in 2002 and 2006, has both won and lost at the Olympics, and he knows what works when coaches compile a team.

"Once they've decided, philosophically, on the kind of team they want to put together, a big part of this job going forward is to make sure that they actually get out and watch these players. I know in 2006, the coaches weren't quite as involved in that process as they were in 2002. We really took a different team that never became a real good team," Quinn explained. "So scouting is very important. Even though we know these guys as NHLers, it's not just about the talent that's available. It's whether that talent can become a team. That's the elusive part; a hard thing to get."

History has proven Quinn right, time and time again. The differences between the 2002 and the 2006 teams on paper were minimal; it was the intangibles that made the 2002 team gold medallists and the 2006 squad seventh-place finishers.

Hockey pundits all point to veterans Mario Lemieux and Steve Yzerman as the difference makers in 2002. At the beginning of the selection process, neither player was in great shape to participate in the Games; Lemieux had chronic back problems, and Yzerman had recurring knee issues. Yet even with all their health concerns, selecting these two players was the best decision for the team. They brought leadership and courage that came to the forefront at the critical moments in the tournament and helped to provide an example for the younger players like Ryan Smyth and Jarome Iginla to look up to.

The team came together around the leadership of Lemieux and Yzerman and made history. Finding that right combination of skills will be a tougher challenge for Steve Yzerman as he now looks at the 2010 team from the other side as Hockey Canada's general manager and director of player operations.

One name that continues to crop up as the potential veteran leader on the team is Joe Sakic. Despite sitting out most of the 2008–09 NHL season with injuries, his leadership skills and talent on the ice are undeniable. Scott Niedermayer is another possible veteran selection who was on the 2002 gold-medal winning team and has been a solid puck-moving defenseman throughout his entire career. On top of these talented veterans, Yzerman has a whole host of other players to choose from.

2010 Olympic Hockey Schedule

Location: Vancouver, BC
Medal Ceremonies: BC Place Stadium

Canada Hockey Place (capacity: 18,630)

February 13: Women, one game
February 16–21: Men's round robin, three games per day
February 22: Women's semifinal, two games
February 23: Men's qualification playoff, three games
February 24: Men's quarterfinal, three games
February 25: Women's medals, two games
February 26: Men's semifinal, two games
February 27: Men's bronze medal, one game
February 28: Men's gold medal game

UBC Thunderbird Arena (capacity: 7200)

February 13–18: Women's round-robin play
February 20: Women's playoff, two games
February 22: Women's playoff, two games
February 23: Men's qualification playoff
February 24: Men's quarterfinal, one game

Chapter Four

Figure Skating

Although Canada has had some early successes in the sport of figure skating, it has only been in the past two decades that Canadian athletes have truly made a name for themselves as a group. Canadian figure skaters first achieved world recognition with the arrival of the grand dame of Canadian figure skating, Barbara Ann Scott. Her gold-medal victory at the 1948 St. Moritz Olympics in Switzerland ushered in a renewed interest among young Canadians to take up the sport. Bursting onto the amateur scene when she was just 11 years old, Barbara Ann Scott reigned supreme not only over the Canadian figure skating scene but also across the globe. She was Canadian junior champion in 1940; senior champion in 1944, 1945, 1946 and 1948; North American Champion from 1945 through to 1947; in 1947 and 1948 she won back-to-back European and World Championships and capped off her amateur career with the Olympic gold.

Since Scott brought Canadian figure skating to the public's attention, other great Canadian champions have come forward, such as pairs figure skaters Barbara Wagner and Robert Paul who beat out a skilled pair from Germany and from the United States to win gold at the 1960 Winter Olympics. However, although there have been a few successes since Barbara Ann Scott's gold in 1948, Canadian figure skaters have not faired well on the Olympic stage until recently.

The arrival of Brian Orser onto the scene brought a new era of interest in the sport, and since his silver-medal performances at the 1984 and 1988 Games, a host of other Canadians have followed in his footsteps, bringing a renewed passion and hope for Canadian figure skating in the Olympics. Such skaters include Kurt Browning, Elvis Stojko, Isabelle Brasseur and Lloyd Eisler, Jamie Sale and David Pelletier, and 2010 hopefuls Patrick Chan and Joannie Rochette.

The Grand Dame of Canadian Figure Skating: Barbara Ann Scott

Anyone who follows Canadian figure skating knows that Barbara Ann Scott is one of the sport's seminal figures. Through her grace on and off the ice, she is known as the queen of Canadian figure skating to this day.

Taking to the ice at seven years old in her hometown of Ottawa, she didn't always have the nicest clothes or skates, but she made do with what she had and quickly began setting herself apart from the other girls on the ice. By 10 years old, Scott was showing real promise as a figure skater, so her parents decided to buy her the best skates on the market. It was a purchase that paid dividends later on.

I can remember when I was 10 years old being in New York being fitted for my first pair of Gustav Stanzione boots. They cost $25 a pair, but they were the best boots money could buy then. Mr. Stanzione told my mother my foot wouldn't grow much more than a half size thereafter. And they didn't. I also had a pair of Wilson blades from England and they cost $15. I wore them all through my amateur and professional skating career.

It was a lot of money at the time for a family of modest means, but by the age of 11, Scott used those same skates to win her first Canadian national junior title.

Two years later, in 1942, she became the first female to land a double lutz in competition.

But her skills on the ice did not come without hard work. She underwent a rigorous training schedule that saw her practice sometimes five to six times a week for eight hours each time. She skated 11 miles (17 kilometres) every day during the winter and practiced her base figures over and over again. Success came at a price, and Barbara Ann Scott was willing to work to get it.

In 1947, not wanting to see her talents relegated to only the Canadian figure skating scene, four of her Ottawa friends raised $10,000 to send Scott, her mother and her coach to the European Championships in Switzerland and the World Championships in Sweden. Scott became the first and last North American figure skater to win the European Championships, and she was the first Canadian to win the world title. At the World's, six of the eight judges put her in first place and two even gave her perfect scores. Her performances on the world stage earned her the Lou Marsh Trophy in 1945, 1947 and 1948, an award given to Canada's top athlete of the year.

With performances on the world stage like those, Scott went into the 1948 Olympics in St. Moritz as the odds-on favourite to win gold, but she was by no means guaranteed the spot.

Up first were the compulsory figures that counted for 60 percent of a skater's overall marks. After completing her program, she was so far ahead of the other women that she could have skated the freestyle program with her eyes closed and still won the gold, but this was an international competition, and anything could happen to take away those chances. On the day of the free skate, she was up against a few challenges. She had to compete with some talented skaters who could surprise given the right opportunity, in particular, four national champions from the countries of England, Austria, Hungary and Czechoslovakia.

The conditions of the ice also left something to be desired. In today's Olympics, athletes have the privilege of skating on temperature-controlled ice in modern indoor arenas. Scott and 25 other skaters had to contend with the freezing Swiss weather on an outdoor rink, and on the day of the competition, the ice had been chopped up by a hockey game that had been played on the ice earlier, and no one had bothered to resurface the rink. To make matters worse, Scott was positioned as the 13th skater and had to skate on an even choppier ice surface. But none of that fazed her. She was the queen of poise, and when it came time for her routine, she nailed every jump, every technical requirement and was the picture of grace and beauty. She easily beat out her competitors to win Canada's first and only gold medal in singles figure skating, female or male.

"My greatest moment in sport was at the Olympics in St. Moritz in 1948. I was on the dais (platform) in a blinding snowstorm. It was between periods of a hockey game. Eva Pawlik of Austria was runner-up with silver and Jeanette Altwegg of Great Britain won bronze," recalled Scott. "I was handed my gold medal in a case. They didn't put it around your neck on a ribbon in those days. Then, our flag was raised on the highest flagpole and our national anthem was played. They played 'O Canada'—so far away from home. It was the proudest moment of my life and tears streamed down my cheeks."

After her victory in St. Moritz, Scott was the toast of the town. She was invited to dinners and galas around the world, from the home of Canada's governor to the steps of the White House, and even to the gate of Buckingham Palace. She was considered the queen of figure skating. When she returned to her hometown of Ottawa, Scott was welcomed back by 70,000 adoring fans—more than one-third of the city's population at the time. The next day, in Toronto, another 70,000 fans turned out to see her when her train pulled into Union Station.

To capitalize on her popularity, the Reliable Toy Company came out with a Barbara Ann Scott doll that they produced from 1948 to 1954. Every little girl who dreamt of gliding across the ice like a ballerina

wanted one of those dolls for Christmas. Selling at
$5.95 a piece, the company pulled in a tidy profit.

After the Olympics, still only 19 years old, Scott
turned pro and began performing in ice skating shows
across Canada, the United States and Great Britain.
She retired from the world of skating in 1955 when she
married Tom King. He was a former All-American
college and NBA player who was director of an entertainment company that was promoting one of Scott's
shows when they first met. In 1991 she was made an
officer of the Order of Canada and in 1998 joined
other athletes and celebrities on Canada's Walk of Fame
in Toronto. She currently lives in Chicago, Illinois.

The Silver of '72

Canada had high hopes for the 1972 Olympics in Sapporo, Japan. But out of the 60 athletes sent overseas to represent the country, only one came back with a medal, and that was Karen Magnussen. It was an incredible triumph for the Vancouver, BC native, considering that she almost did not make it to the Olympics in the first place.

Bursting onto the Canadian figure skating scene in 1965 with a win at the National Junior Championships, Magnussen was Canada's most promising talent. Her fluidity on the ice was equally matched by her athleticism. The country watched as she blossomed into Canada's best hope on the international scene. After winning the Canadian Championships in 1968 and again in 1969, Magnussen made the jump onto the world stage with a second-place finish at the North American Championships in 1969.

Just when everything was going well, she began to notice that she was having trouble in her routines and soon it became painful just to walk. Despite the pain, she travelled to Colorado for the 1969 World Championship fully intending to go for the gold, but the pain had gotten to the point where she could no longer bear it, and a doctor had to be called in. After a few tests and x-rays, it was discovered that she had stress fractures in both her legs. The doctors gave her the bad news that she would not be able to participate in the World Championship, and that if her fractures didn't heal properly, she might have to forget about figure skating for good.

The news was a devastating blow to Magnussen, who had just turned 17. But the years of dedicated practice had finally caught up with her. Beginning at the age of 12, Magnussen had practiced seven hours a day, 42 hours per week, for 40 weeks. Aside from figure skating, she was also enrolled in ballet classes and was a regular jogger on the roads around her house. The constant jumping on hard ice combined with the running and training took a toll on her legs and caused vertical stress cracks in the bones.

"It was frustrating. Especially after all the hard training," recalled Magnussen. "I suddenly went from seven hours a day to nothing. It's amazing how your muscles almost go to putty."

It was a difficult time for Magnussen who was not used to a relaxed pace, but the time off enabled her to focus on her goals once she healed and to mentally prepare for the ultimate stage for a figure skater, the Olympics. With determination and patience, she recovered by the spring of 1970 and was ready to test out her legs at the Canadian Championship. Not missing a step, she won back her Canadian title in 1970 and repeated that feat again in 1971. She was back in fighting form and was prepared to take on the world.

Magnussen followed her Canadian title with a gold-medal performance at the North American Figure

Skating Championships and a third-place finish at the World's. After winning the Canadian Championships again in 1972, she was ready for her Olympic debut. Her biggest challenge of the Olympics would be beating her longtime rival, American Janet Lynn.

At the 1972 Games in Sapporo, the figure skating event was divided into the freestyle skate and the compulsory figures, each worth 50 percent of the overall score. Up first was the compulsory skate. Magnussen and Janet Lynn both did well, but it was the tall, graceful Austrian Beatrix Schuba who built up a commanding lead over the Canadian and the American. Schuba was widely acknowledged as the best practitioner of the compulsory figures in the history of the sport. To have any hopes of making up lost ground in the compulsories, Magnussen had to perform the best freestyle program of her life and hope that Schuba took a tumble or two.

Magnussen put in a great performance, landing every jump and completing every required move. At the end of the freestyle skate, she was in first place while Janet Lynn was second. Beatrix Schuba finished well out, in seventh place, but her numbers from the compulsory figures were so high that she still finished in the gold-medal position. Magnussen had to settle for silver. Lynn was left with the bronze

A public outrage quickly followed the event. Television audiences worldwide only saw the free skate portion of the event, which Magnussen clearly dominated, and missed out on the dull and lengthy compulsory figures in which Schuba had received such high scores. The world felt that Magnussen was robbed of the title that she deserved. After all, they had seen her perform breathtaking double axels and split leaps, whereas Schuba appeared to be merely an amateur in Lynn and Magnussen's shadow.

A growing dissatisfaction with figure skating's governing body arose out of the controversy. It resulted in a change in how the marks were awarded for the compulsory figures. Figure skating is a sport that is almost made for television. Viewers can capture the artistry and athleticism of the skaters up close. In other sports, such as football, fans don't get to see the players' faces. Figure skating is big league, and the compulsories were making people switch the channel.

Canada, nevertheless, savoured Magnussen's silver medal because none of the 60 other athletes who were sent to the Games came home with a medal. But as nice as the silver medal was for Canada, Magnussen wanted to prove that she was the best in the world. In 1973, the International Skating Union introduced changes to competitive rules that saw the addition of the short program and a free skate component with required jumping, spinning and footwork elements (which accounted for 20 percent of the overall score, with the free skating "long program" still counting for half the total score, and compulsory figures were reduced to 30 percent of the total mark). The change in rules cleared the path for Magnussen to head to the top of the podium.

At the 1973 World Championships in Bratislava, Czechoslovakia, Magnussen performed a perfect short program that put her so far ahead of rival Janet Lynn—who had fallen twice during her short program to place 12th—that Magnussen coasted through both the long and the compulsory programs to win gold.

British journalist Clive James commented on Magnussen's win:

> *In the compulsories Janet Lynn had mucked up her double jump and left Karen Magnussen too far ahead to catch. With the competitive element eliminated, the spirit of the art was free to flourish and Magnussen turned in an absolute face-freezer—a display of dramatic power that ran like cold fury on silver rails, propelled by one continuous friction-free impulse from her eloquently stacked center section.*

Magnussen had achieved her world title at the age of 21. She turned professional and toured with the Ice Capades for several years before switching her attention to the next generation of figure skaters. She launched the Karen Magnussen Foundation to help train and support talented young Canadian skaters. She coached other notable Canadian figure skaters such as Elizabeth Manley and Josée Chouinard.

Canadian Sweetheart: Elizabeth Manley

Prior to the 1988 Winter Olympics in Calgary, the figure skating world's attention was focused on the top two women in the sport, East German Katarina Witt and American Debi Thomas. Ottawa native Elizabeth Manley did not figure into the projections as a possible gold medallist. Manley herself was simply hoping for a top-six finish and maybe a medal as the ultimate prize.

How could the Ottawa native think she had a chance against the likes of Witt and Thomas when even her own hometown newspaper, *The Ottawa Citizen,* had written her off as inconsistent and as having no chance of matching the performances of the world's top figure skaters? Luckily for Canada, Manley did not listen to any of her naysayers.

In the first part of the three-part competition, battling the last days of a bad flu as well as being out of practice, Manley managed to finish in fourth place, much to everyone's surprise.

In the short program, she was still feeling the effects of her flu and had to fight an extreme case of the nerves, but once she was out on the ice and the music started blaring, Manley put on the performance of a lifetime, landing all her jumps and nailing all the technical requirements. Her short program success vaulted her into third place, putting her into serious contention for the gold. But as good as her short program was, Manley saved her best for last.

From the first note of the music of her long program, Manley's confidence was palpable to the audience gathered at Calgary's Saddledome. She performed each element of her routine with flawless grace. With each successful completion, the crowd's cheers got louder and louder. Even some of the American fans could not help but cheer on Canada's newly discovered sweetheart. During her complete routine she pulled off five flawless triple jumps.

When Manley ended her program at centre ice, she put her hands to her face in disbelief at the performance she had just given. It was absolutely flawless, and the judges agreed. She finished first place in the long program and vaulted into second place, good enough for the silver medal. Manley had defied the odds and earned a spot in the hearts of all Canadians that day. She continued to perform in front of audiences across North America with the Ice Capades for several years and now works as a figuring skating coach and media commentator.

Dreams Dashed

To say a media circus surrounded the 1994 Olympic women's figure skating event is to put it lightly. The entire world was watching the event because of what had occurred a few weeks earlier at the U.S. Figure Skating Championships. And this media circus would end up affecting the Olympics of one unfortunate Canadian skater.

Tonya Harding had gotten used to being on top of the figure skating world. She had won the 1991 U.S. Championship and finished second at the World's that same year, but another rising American figure skating star named Nancy Kerrigan was threatening to steal some of Harding's limelight. Winning meant everything to Harding, and at the 1994 U.S. Championships she proved that she was willing to do anything to stay at the top.

On January 6, 1994, at a practice session for the U.S. Championships, Kerrigan was attacked by a stranger who struck her on the knee with a crowbar. The attack took her out of contention for the U.S. Championships and conveniently left Harding as one of the top favourites. Harding ended up winning the event, while Kerrigan was forced to withdraw because of her knee injury.

After the competition, it surfaced that Harding had planned the attack and hired someone to carry out the assault. She was stripped of her title, but when the U.S. Olympic Committee tried to have her removed from the Olympic team, she threatened to sue and was allowed to participate at the Games in Lillehammer.

At the Olympics, Canadian figure skater Josée Chouinard tried to stay out of the way of the media that was following Tonya Harding, but she could not avoid her forever. In the middle of skating her long program, Harding suddenly stopped, went to the officials bench in tears and pleaded with the event staff to be given some time to replace a broken lace on her skates. To the amazement of everyone at the arena, Harding was allowed the extra time to fix her skate. However, because Harding took extra time, the next skater was forced to rush onto the ice ill-prepared for this sudden turn of events. That skater was Canada's Josée Chouinard.

In typical Canadian fashion, no one complained at the lack of fairness, but the three stumbles in Chouinard's long program can at least be partly blamed on Harding's broken lace. Chouinard had her Olympic dreams dashed when she finished out of medal contention.

Years later, it must have put a smile on Chouinard's face when she turned on the television and saw that Harding had signed on to Fox Channel's reality TV show *Celebrity Boxing*.

Elvis Is in the Building

For Canadian skating fans, the 1994 Games were one of the most anticipated Olympics in recent memory. Canada had always done well in Olympic figure skating but was never as dominant a force as the Americans or the Russians. That is not to say that there were no great triumphs in our Olympic figure skating history; after all, Barbara Ann Scott single-handedly put Canadian figure skating on the map, but Canadian male athletes had always fallen short of the gold podium.

The closest Canada had come to a figure skating superstar in the male arena was in Brian Orser. Back in 1984 at the Winter Games in Sarajevo and in 1988 before a home crowd in Calgary, he won silver medals in the men's singles event. Canada's previous best placing had been a bronze at 1960 Games won by Donald Jackson and another bronze at the 1976 Games won by the graceful Toller Cranston. But with the arrival of Brian Orser, the world was finally forced to see that Canada could produce more than just great hockey players. Following in Orser's footsteps were two young Canadians who brought excitement back to Canada's Olympic skating program and could challenge the world's best. Going into the 1994 Lillehammer Games in Norway, Kurt Browning and Elvis Stojko weren't given any chances of winning gold, but the Canadians were not going down without a fight.

The two young men would have their work cut out for them, however. American Brian Boitano returned to see if he could repeat his gold-medal performance from the 1988 Olympics in Calgary. Russian Viktor Petrenko had taken the gold medal at the 1992 Albertville Olympics and wanted to add to his collection as well. France's Philippe Candeloro and American champion Scott Davis were also gunning for the top spot. To make it into the top five, both Browning and Stojko would need to achieve their personal bests. The Canadians were no slouches.

Browning, a four-time world champ and reigning world title-holder, had never won a medal in the two previous Olympics, but going into Lillehammer, he was determined to make his mark.

"This time of my life quite possibly will never be duplicated," he said just before his first performance in Lillehammer. "The excitement, the pressure, the expectations. Stepping out on the ice and knowing the whole world is watching. If I can just make everybody remember something. Give them something so they won't forget."

A diminutive Canadian had also travelled to the Olympics to challenge for the top spot. Elvis Stojko was riding high after his recent defeat over Kurt Browning at the Canadian Championships, but there was some speculation on whether the world was ready for his unique perspective on figure skating. While other performers chose more refined routines backed by the music of the classical masters, Stojko's program was based around the music from the biopic of Bruce Lee called *Dragon,* and Stojko's moves on the ice mimicked the style of the martial arts he had practiced since he was a child. Technically, he was a master, but he had always lost points on artistry. It remained to be seen whether the world would understand his new approach to such a traditional sport.

But before even lacing up his skates, Stojko's outlook on the 1994 Winter Games was positive.

If two Canadian flags get up in the podium, I think it will be the biggest thing that has ever happened in figure skating. You know, Kurt and I do our own things as individuals and we compete hard against each other but in the end I hope we're gonna be up there together. That would make it perfect.

Brian Boitano was the first skater to perform in the technical program, and right from the start things went horribly wrong for him. Looking almost lost on the ice, he fell on his first attempt at a triple axel and could not complete the required series of combinations. At the end of the evening, the once king of the ice was in eighth place. Viktor Petrenko, the reigning gold medallist, did much worse and ended up in ninth place. With all of the old pros falling to the wayside, it was the perfect chance for Stojko to seize the spotlight.

Elvis was up next after Petrenko. Stojko was no stranger to the Olympics, having competed at the 1992 Albertville Games in France and coming in seventh place. Canadian figure skating fans felt he got a raw deal at those Games, insisting that the judges did not appreciate his modern, athletic take on figure skating. Lillehammer was Stojko's chance to prove that he belonged among the best in the world and was not just some Canadian flash in the pan.

Stojko's performance was near perfect. He landed every jump and flowed through every move, giving the judges everything they expected and more. When the scores flashed on the board at the end of his routine, Stojko had taken over first place.

However, his spot at the top did not last long. Russia's Aleksei Urmanov was flawless in his routine. Whereas Stojko's routine was energetic and fiery, Urmanov's was classical and sensuous. He could jump with the best of the skaters, and his artistic performance was sure to merit quality marks. During his skate, he capped his performance off with a triple axel, double toe combination that wowed the crowd and raised a few of the judges' eyebrows. Urmanov's marks hit the board and were ahead of Stojko. France's Philippe Candeloro skated after Urmanov to a third-place finish. The only skater remaining was Canada's Kurt Browning.

Wearing a black shirt and black pants, Browning skated out to centre ice and waited for his music to start. If he demonstrated to the judges his famous dramatic flair and landed every jump, he could make it into a medal position; tough but not impossible. From the outset, things appeared to be going his way. He landed a jump he had missed at the 1992 Games in Albertville, but everything he did after that jump was a complete disaster. He fell on a triple flip, then turned a required double axel into a single. His dreams of an Olympic medal were done. The judges put him in 12th place. After his performance, Browning was interviewed by the Canadian media and apologized to Canadians for disappointing them. "It's all over. Maybe it wasn't meant to be."

But the medals had yet to be handed out. Athletes still had the free skate program to make up any lost ground. Browning was too far out to hope for a medal; he was simply skating for his pride. Dressed in a white jacket and black bow tie, he skated to the music from the movie *Casablanca*. Playing the role of Rick Blaine, he captured the crowd's attention by exhibiting his natural charm and wit on the ice. At the end of the program, he had not skated his best ever but had captured the world's notice with a courageous performance. The judges agreed with the crowd's assessment and awarded him marks that catapulted him all the way to a fifth-place finish.

Of the top three skaters after the technical program, Stojko was the first to hit the ice. Skating that night to the music of the biographical film of *Dragon*, Stojko looked like a man on a mission. His moves on the ice were performed with the elegance and style of a seasoned veteran. The highlight of his routine came when he perfectly landed a triple axel, toe combination that had the crowd cheering.

When Stojko finished his program, skating fans knew that he had just completed something special and might even become the first Canadian to win a gold medal in figure skating. Stojko received top marks for the technical side of his program, but on the artistic front, a Russian judge gave him a 5.5 score. It seemed the old prejudices against his modern take on figure skating were again coming back. He had secured himself a medal; now it was up to Russia's Aleksei Urmanov to decide what colour it would be.

Urmanov skated a beautiful program, but it wasn't without its mistakes. On a triple flip, he tripped on the landing and almost hit the boards. Stojko had not faltered once during his program. What would the judges do? Urmanov's marks came up, and he was awarded the gold. Stojko ended up with the silver. It was an incredible accomplishment for the Canadian skater, but in some ways he felt wronged by the Russian judge's mark of 5.5. But Stojko remained humble in his response.

As soon as I started the program, right through to the end, I skated free. Nothing can take that away from me, no matter what a judge says or people think. It's a matter of opinion. It's the best skate I've ever had under such circumstances. I challenged myself and I won.

Since retirement Stojko has performed in professional ice shows across North America and has embarked on a singing and acting career. He can still be seen on television as a commentator during skating events.

Scandal!

It seems that every Winter Olympic Games has its moment of controversy when it comes to the figure skating event, but no one was prepared for the scandal that rocked the 2002 Salt Lake City Winter Games and the Canadian pair of Jamie Sale and David Pelletier.

The story of pairs skaters Jamie Sale and David Pelletier almost never happened. Back in 1996 while Pelletier was selling hot dogs at the Molson Centre and Sale worked in a coffee shop in Montréal, the two young figure skating athletes were both searching for partners who could complement their styles. When someone suggested that they should meet, the two strangers decided to test the proverbial waters together on the ice. It was not a match made in heaven, but rather, the classic clash of personalities, and the partnership never got off the ground.

"Maybe I was a little more of a jerk in 1996, and maybe she was too much of a Miss Pretty," Pelletier later recalled.

The two quickly parted ways and were perfectly content with never seeing each other again. Sale returned to singles skating but because of injuries was never able to achieve the success that she wanted. Pelletier partnered up at different times with Allison Gaylor and Caroline Roy, but he never placed higher than sixth place in any competition. With his career seemingly headed nowhere, Pelletier's coach Richard Gauthier suggested he give Jamie Sale another try. Reluctantly, the two met up again in Edmonton in February 1998, and this time there was an immediate connection.

"The first time we grabbed hands, it was just great," said Pelletier.

One month later, they were both living and training together in Montréal on a regular basis. The partnership was going so well that one year later, the pair won their first international competition at Skate America, finishing ahead of the two-time reigning world champions Yelena Berezhnaya and Anton Sikharulidze of Russia. Prior to the 2002 Salt Lake Olympics, Sale and Pelletier managed to build up a nine-event winning streak, including three wins over Yelena and Anton, whose careers were taking a turn for the worse.

With the pressure increasing on the Russian pair to win, Yelena tried to get an edge on the competition by taking performance-enhancing drugs. She tested positive after winning the 2000 European Championships, and she and her partner were stripped of the title and barred from participating in the World Championships taking place that same year. The Russian pair was struggling and looking to the 2002 Olympics to get their careers back on track. As the Games approached, world rankings had the Russians, the Chinese pair of Xue Shen and Hongbo Zhao and Canada's Sale and Pelletier as the top medal contenders.

Pressure on Sale and Pelletier to bring home the gold was intense. They were seen as the only hope of breaking the Russians' hold on the event that had endured for more than 40 years. Canada had won only two gold medals in figure skating history, and Sale and Pelletier were the country's best hope in a long time. When it came time for the short program, all eyes of the world were on the Canadian and Russian pairs to see how they would deal with the pressure.

Up first was Berezhnaya and Sikharulidze. From the moment they hit the arena floodlights, it was clear that something was not right with Yelena. It turned out that upon arriving in Utah, the pair had taken a daylong snowmobiling trip into the mountains, and the dry mountain air had left Yelena's skin chapped, and she was in pain. In an attempt to heal her skin, Yelena had gone to a tanning salon, which only made matters worse. She took to the ice for the short program donning a brilliant orange glow, but she and Anton managed to skate a near flawless program that set the tone for the competition. Despite their past problems and Yelena's painful skin condition, the Russians had come to compete.

When Sale and Pelletier hit the ice they delivered a near-perfect performance as well, but after taking their final pose, Pelletier slipped, sending both him and Sale sprawling to the ice. The mistake dropped the Canadian pair to second place behind their Russian rivals. But the scores were still close. The gold medal would have to be decided after the long program.

On the day of the long program, tensions were running high in the arena. Although it was possible that the Chinese skaters could surprise everyone with a flawless performance, oddsmakers had the battle for gold set between the Russians and the Canadians. But during the warm-ups for the free skate, an accident threatened to derail all the hard work the skaters had done to get to this place in the competition.

With about one minute left in warm-ups, Berezhnaya and Sikharulidze appeared to be getting ready to do a throw jump, when Sale slammed into Anton. Sale put her hands up to try to avoid the collision, but it did little good because she was skating at full speed.

As both skaters went crashing to the ice, Anton's skate clipped Sale's knee. For a few moments she stayed down on her knee with her head bowed. Sikharulidze skated over and asked if she was okay. Pelletier darted over to his partner's side and helped her off the ice.

"It really shook me up, it knocked the wind out of me," said Sale immediately after the accident. "I looked at Dave (Pelletier) and I thought, 'I'm not finished. No way.' Adrenaline does amazing things for you. I was—as I'm sure they were—I was in some pain in my stomach. My arms kind of started to get a little bit numb. So when I stepped on the ice, I just said, 'I'm not giving up.'

I looked at Dave and said, 'This is for us and I'm not giving up.'"

Although the accident seemed to provide Sale and Pelletier with extra energy, the incident appeared to have thrown the Russian pair off their game. Berezhnaya and Sikharulidze skated a beautiful routine to the music of "Meditation from Thais," but there were several noticeable errors during their program, including Sikharulidze stumbling on a double axel landing. When the pair completed their routine, their technical score suffered a little because of the stumbles but remained questionably high, with seven 5.9s (6.0 being perfect).

It was thought that if the Russian pair had scored so high with a flawed routine, then surely if the Canadian pair skated a flawless routine they would also be awarded high marks. Sale and Pelletier skated to the theme of *Love Story*, a tale of two college kids who had fallen in love and suffered tragedy. Aside from landing all their jumps, the pair's routine had the crowd standing on its feet once Sale and Pelletier came to a stop in the middle of the arena. The crowd began chanting, "Six, Six, Six!"

When their marks hit the board, however, the judges' opinions seemingly differed from that of the rest of the world watching. Of the nine judges, five had voted in favour of the Russians. The five judges were from Russia, China, Poland, Ukraine and France. The arena erupted into a chorus of boos. The Canadian Olympic

Committee (COC) immediately put in a complaint with the International Skating Union that they launch an investigation into the judging. The COC did not want the Russians to be stripped of the gold; they just wanted the results to be accurate. According to COC president Michael Chambers, "We are not here to pull someone down. We are here to pull someone up." The focus of the investigation quickly centred on the French judge Marie-Reine Le Gougne, whose vote was the one that appeared to give the Russians the gold.

Le Gougne began her career as a figure skater in 1973 and later turned to judging. Over the next 15 years, she became a well-respected judge but was also very critical of the biases in the system. Weeks before the Olympics, she was quoted as blasting the skating world and the embedded corruption. Speaking about the pressure to support skaters from a judge's home country, she said, "One is stuck between a rock and a hard place. We're here to push our skater, but without contravening the ethics and risking suspension." Unfortunately, she did not stick to her words.

After many accusations and finger pointing, Le Gougne finally cracked and admitted that she had traded her first-place vote to the Russians for a first-place vote for a French ice dancer. Russian organized crime was implicated in the affair, and there were allegations that the scandal would also implicate six other judges.

For her part, Le Gougne was barred from judging competitions for the next three years.

During the entire investigation, Sale and Pelletier were international stars. Every media outlet wanted to hear their story, and soon the controversy began to overshadow the rest of the Olympics. In order to put the matter to rest and right the wrong done to the Canadian pair, IOC president Jacques Rogge awarded the Canadian pair a gold medal as well.

Sale and Pelletier were happy to receive their gold medals but were also anxious to put the media circus behind them. For their part, the pair had no ill feelings towards the Russian skaters.

"Dave and I have just really moved on. We moved on even right after [the Games]. As far as we're concerned, we did our job and that's all that matters. We're moving on to bigger and better things and we're trying not to become involved because it really has nothing to do with us besides the fact that it was our event," Sale said in an interview on NBC's *Today Show*. "It's good to see that this is coming out maybe, but is it really good for our sport," she added.

Patrick Chan

Patrick Chan began his obsession with figure skating at five years old in his hometown of Ottawa, Ontario. He began distinguishing himself on the national stage at the age of 13 when he won the Canadian pre-novice title. He followed his first major title with a win again in 2004 on the national stage, taking the novice title, and another win at the 2005 Canadian Junior Championship. Winning the Canadian junior title earned him a spot on the national junior squad and a trip to the World Juniors. Then only 14 years old, he was the youngest skater ever to compete in the juniors. For his first international major competition, the young Canadian placed seventh overall. The incredible poise and calm he showed under pressure truly displayed the heart of a champion, and he was being called Canada's next great hope.

But his career was nearly taken off track when his longtime coach Osbourne Colson died in July 2006. It was a difficult time for the young skater who had looked upon Colson not just as a coach but also as somewhat of a father figure. Chan took some time off skating to mourn the loss of his coach and slowly returned to active competition.

After competing in several more junior level tournaments in 2007, he moved up to the senior level and competed in his first Canadian Figure Skating Championship, placing seventh. Just one year later he returned to the Canadian Championships and won the title. At just 17 years old he was the youngest Canadian to win the title. In 2009, he successfully defended his title as Canadian champion.

With a reputation firmly established on the Canadian skating scene, Chan set his sights on the world. After placing second at the 2009 Four Continents Championships, he made his inaugural appearance at the 2009 World Figure Skating Championship as one of the favourites to take home a medal.

Chan's choreographer, Lori Nichol, had nothing but good things to say about her protégé going into the World's:

He's fresh and full of life and he represents freedom and abandonment in skating. He has such mastery of his blades and of all the things blades can do, but he's also incredibly strong and so he can take it to all sorts of levels he's only discovering now. For me, when somebody has that kind of strength and mastery of the actual skill of skating…he has the real essence of skating and when he keeps letting that out more and more, it's going to be remarkable.

Chan's well-honed skills and mastery on his blades helped him to second place behind American Evan Lysacek. Up next for the young Canadian champion is to place his name in the history books and become the first Canadian male figure skater to win gold at the Vancouver Olympics in 2010.

Joannie Rochette

Montréal native Joannie Rochette got her start at the Olympics in 2006 when she came in fifth place. It was an excellent placing for the 23-year-old Canadian's first Olympics, but that was just the beginning.

Since starting her lifelong passion with figure skating, Rochette has been on a steady climb to the top of the figure skating world. To date, her greatest triumph has most certainly been her performance at the 2009 World Figure Skating Championship. Although she was one of the top female skaters going into the tournament, the competition was fierce, and Rochette had her work cut out for her if she was going to come away with a medal. Japan's Miki Ando and Mao Asada and South Korea's Kim Yu-Na were among the early favourites in the competitions and were well known for their solid artistic performances. Rochette had a good program, but her strong suit was the technical side. After the women's short program, she surprised all by coming in second overall. But her position on the podium was not guaranteed; Mao Asada was just a few points behind. In the long program, Rochette managed to hang on with a third-place finish and second place overall. It was the first time a Canadian woman had won a medal at the World Championships since Elizabeth Manley's win in 1988.

"This is unbelievable, it's been so, so long and now to be able to deliver it…" Rochette said. "For myself, I'm so, so happy to do it, it's my little girl's dream, since I was very young I've been dreaming about that. I just hope to inspire some young girls who want to achieve big things in skating and make them believe it's possible," she added. "They know my history and know that five years ago no one would have thought—or even three years ago—that I would be on the podium, that I had the talent to be on it. But through hard work, I think anything is possible and I proved that to myself and hopefully proved that to all the other Canadian ladies."

Going into the 2010 Olympics, Rochette is one of Canada's best hopes to bring home a medal.

2010 Olympic Figure Skating Schedule

Location: Vancouver, BC
Medal Ceremonies: BC Place Stadium

Pacific Coliseum, Hastings Park (capacity: 14,239)

February 14: Pairs short program
February 15: Pairs free skate
February 16: Men's short program
February 18: Men's free skate
February 19: Ice-dancing compulsories
February 21: Ice-dancing original dance
February 22: Ice-dancing free dance
February 23: Women's short program
February 25: Women's free skate
February 27: Exhibition skate

Chapter Five

Speed Skating

People first got the idea to strap blades to their feet to help them glide over ice more than 1000 years ago, most likely on the canals and waterways of Scandinavia and the Netherlands. Not having any stainless steel at their disposal, men laced animal bones to their footwear and glided across the frozen lakes and canals. What started out as a tool to help with the hunt soon developed into a useful and enjoyable means of transportation for the Dutch, and as time passed, the first skate designs began to emerge.

It was actually a Scotsman who, in 1592, first shaped an iron blade that was specifically made for skating. Soon after, skating clubs began to spring up all around Europe, and by 1763 the world's first organized speed skating race was held in Fens, England.

Eventually, speed skating made its way across the pond and onto the rivers and lakes of the Great White North. Canada's first recorded speed skating event took place on the St. Lawrence River in 1854 when three British Army officers raced from Montréal to Québec City. With so many bodies of water available, from frozen rivers and lakes to ponds and creeks, Canada produced many high-quality speed skating athletes.

Canada's first Olympic speed skating medals were won at the 1932 Winter Olympics in Lake Placid, New York. The count by the closing ceremony was one silver and four bronze. They would be Canada's only speed skating medals until the 1952 Games in Oslo, Norway, when Gordon Audley won bronze in the 500-metre event. By the late 1930s, popular interest in the sport began to decline as more and more young people took to hockey. The advent of World War II also saw speed skating popularity decline. In 1932, Canada had its chance to seize the reins as the world's best in speed skating, but by 1952 Norway emerged as the dominant country. It wasn't until the 1984 Olympics when Gaetan Boucher captured two gold medals that interest in speed skating once again took centre stage in Canada.

The short track speed skaters were the first to make a name for Canada on the international stage. A plethora of short track skaters suddenly emerged out of Québec and began to dominate the ice. Skaters such as Sylvie Daigle, Nathalie Lambert and Marc Gagnon started winning races all over the world and at the Olympics. The long track skaters took a little longer to make an appearance, but by the 1998 Games, athletes such as Catriona Le May Doan, Jeremy Wotherspoon and Cindy Klassen began to make inroads on the international stage. As Vancouver 2010 fast approaches, Canada will look to solidify its position in the sport in front of a supportive home crowd.

Québec Speedster Gaetan Boucher

When Gaetan Boucher began speed skating as a young man, there were little to no facilities in Canada in which he could practice. Canada was well behind the rest of the world in speed skating at the time. For most of his career Boucher was forced to practice in rinks designed specifically for hockey or had to live in Europe and practice on their artificial ice ovals. But the determined athlete from Charlesbourg, Québec, did not let the obstacles get in his way.

Although he had begun to make a name for himself in the late '70s, appearing at the 1976 Winter Games in Innsbruck, Austria, Boucher was still young and unable to keep up with the world-class athletes. However, just four years later, the world took notice at the 1980 Winter Games in Lake Placid, New York, when Gaetan took home the first Canadian men's medal in speed skating since 1952 by winning silver in the 1000-metre event. Just one year later, he set a new world record in the 1000 metres with a time of 1:13.39 seconds. Although that record has since been beaten by several seconds, at that time, Boucher's time was very fast.

But Boucher wanted more, and he predicted that at the 1984 Winter Games in Sarajevo, he would walk away with more medals. In his first race, the 500-metre sprint, he was expected to do well, though taking the gold was still out in the open. Boucher finished in third place and took home the bronze medal for his efforts. But this was not good enough. He wanted more. After all, the 500 metre wasn't his specialty.

Boucher was a 1000-metre technical genius, knowing exactly when to push hard and when to push even harder. But conditions at the outdoor arena in Sarajevo were less than ideal. The city was plagued by some of the worst air-pollution levels in Europe, which made it difficult for the high-performance athletes to perform at their best. But despite the challenges, Boucher went on to win the gold medal over Soviet Sergey Khlebnikov by eight-tenths of a second, which might not sound like much, but in speed skating it is a large margin. Three days later, Boucher again beat the Soviet skater in the 1500 metre by a half second. Gaetan Boucher the speed skating legend was born.

He continued to skate up until the 1988 Winter Games in Calgary, but he will always be remembered for capturing the world's attention at the 1984 Sarajevo Winter Games.

Gaetan Boucher's third medal at the 1984 Winter Olympics put him into the record books as Canada's greatest Winter Games athlete of the 20th century; a Winter Olympics record that would not be broken until Cindy Klassen won five medals at the 2006 Winter Games in Turino, Italy.

Super Skater Catriona Le May Doan

After having just come off the 1998 Speed Skating World Championships in Calgary where she won gold in the 500-metre event and a silver in the 1000 metres, Catriona Le May Doan of Saskatoon, Saskatchewan, was one of Canada's favourites to come away with a medal at the 1998 Olympics in Nagano, Japan. As well as her World Championship status, she was also the holder of the 500-metre world record. In November 1997 in Calgary, she became the first woman to break the 38-second mark in the 500-metre event, skating to a finishing time of 37.90 seconds. Before the year was over, she would break her own record and set the bar at 37.55 seconds.

Le May Doan had participated in her first Olympic Games in Lillehammer, Norway, in 1994. It was a major moment in any athlete's career, but the young skater was far from ready for the pressure of the world stage. At that point in her career she was a solid, talented skater on the Canadian national circuit but had yet to make any significant inroads internationally. It was in between the 1994 and 1998 Olympics that she began training with 1994 silver medallist Susan Auch. Under the guidance of Susan's brother, Derrick, Le May Doan began shaving seconds off her times, and by 1997, was considered one of the fastest in the sport.

With Le May Doan, Susan Auch and men's skater Jeremy Wotherspoon, Canada had a formidable team for the 1998 Olympics. Just a few weeks before the Games, the Europeans were starting to take notice of the athletes coming out of Canada. Norwegian journalist Mette Bugge had nothing but praise for the Canadians as the Games approached: "Canada has always had one or two good skaters. But now it is a full team, and Canada is becoming one of the big speed skating countries." Such high praises from a country that had dominated the sport for many of the Olympic Games showed just how far the Canadian program had come. Little did they know that Catriona Le May Doan was about to take Canadian speed skating to a whole new level.

On February 14, 1998, wearing the colour of Valentine's Day, Le May Doan laced up her skates for the 500-metre event. There were huge expectations on Le May Doan because she had just won the World Championship in the same event a few weeks before the start of the Olympics. In Nagano, she had already made it through the opening rounds with relative ease, but the competition was heating up, and she would not get a free pass to the gold. Japanese skater Tomomi Okazaki had posted the fastest time of the day, and the home crowd roared their appreciation. As Okazaki passed by the crowds, she put her finger to her lips, gesturing that the crowd be quiet as the next athletes set up for the last race. The final pairing was Le May Doan and her Canadian training partner Susan Auch.

The Canadian skaters were each other's toughest rivals and greatest supporters at the same time. At the 1998 World Championships where Le May Doan won the gold in the 500 metres, it was Auch who came in second. Training together on a daily basis, the two skaters had developed an almost identical skating style, and their lap times at various distances were only separated by fractions of a second.

Standing on the line before the eager crowds in Nagano and waiting for the gun to sound, both Canadians wanted to win, but neither would be upset to lose to the other. The crowd, respecting Okazaki's wishes, fell eerily silent just before the start. Le May Doan and Auch blasted through the first 100 metres of the race exchanging the lead several times. Coming into the final push, Auch had a slight lead on Le May Doan, but the wily skater found some reserve energy and turned on the afterburners. It was close, but Le May Doan crossed the line first. Looking over at the clock, Le May Doan saw that she had taken the gold medal and Auch had the silver.

"I was genuinely happy to see her win," said Auch, "to see her arms raised when she crossed the line."

"What a great race," said Le May Doan after the win. "Susan really pushed me. I had to tell myself that I was the strongest skater out there and trust that I could make up the ground on the back stretch."

Catriona Le May Doan accepted her gold medal with pride, and tears came to her eyes as the Canadian flag was raised and "O Canada" blared over the speakers. It was Canada's first individual gold medal in long track speed skating since Gaetan Boucher had won double gold at the Sarajevo Olympics in 1984. As she was making her way off the podium through the throng of reporters, one reporter asked her how she was going to celebrate. "Now I can relax a bit," she answered. "Then it'll be time to get ready for the next race."

Just a few days later she skated in the 1000-metre event and won a bronze medal for her efforts. Winning one medal was the goal, but coming away with two was more than she had anticipated. She became an instant star in Canada and a media darling, but her odyssey on the ice was far from over.

After the 1998 Olympics, she took some time off to enjoy her win but was immediately back on the ice at the Olympic oval in Calgary. She returned to defend her World Championship title in the 500-metre event in 1999 and again in 2001. Now into her 30s, she still was not showing any signs of slowing down and continued to train for her final appearance at the Olympics in 2002.

Just prior to the start of the 2002 Salt Lake City Games, Le May Doan was given the honour of carrying the Canadian flag at the opening ceremonies of the Games. It was a proud moment for the speed skater, but it did not come without controversy. Prior to the Games, many Canadian athletes had openly requested not to be nominated for the job of flag bearer because the duties behind it can take up a lot of the athlete's time and energy, with a full day of ceremonies, interviews and photo sessions. Hockey broadcaster and overly proud Canadian Don Cherry had his own opinion: "I'm sure in the United States they don't have that problem, they'd be proud to carry the flag," said Cherry. "They're up there representing the country... they should be ashamed of themselves."

Despite Cherry's remarks, even the director of Speed Skating Canada, Emery Holmik, supported certain athletes' decisions. "The opening ceremonies are a tiring enough process. If you add all the demands of being flag-bearer and with a relatively heavy racing schedule, taking on that extra task is, as they've correctly evaluated, too great a load."

Angered by the controversy, Canada's pick for flag bearer also weighed in on the subject. "Anytime that someone questions the pride that you have in representing your country, I take offense to it," Le May Doan said. "Every athlete should take offense to it."

There was also the supposed curse that accompanied the flag bearer throughout the Games. Jean-Luc Brassard carried the flag at the 1998 Games and failed to medal; the same thing happened to Kurt Browning who went into the 1994 Games with hopes for a medal but after a disastrous opening he failed to make the podium. Yet despite the added responsibility, media attention and threats of a curse, Le May Doan walked at the front of the Canadian contingent with the flag proudly in her hands. Paying no attention to talk of a curse, she also went on to defend her title as the 500-metre speed skating champ, bringing home another gold medal.

Catriona Le May Doan retired from skating in 2003, and in 2004 she gave birth to her first child, Greta, with husband Bart Doan, cousin of NHL hockey player Shane Doan. Her life continues to revolve around sports, working for several years as a CBC commentator during the Olympics. In 2005 she was inducted into the Canadian Sports Hall of Fame and was named an officer of the Order of Canada.

The Fastest: Cindy Klassen

Winnipeg, Manitoba, native Cindy Klassen is Canada's most decorated all-time Olympian, and she isn't finished competing yet. Owner of six Olympic speed skating medals, Klassen fell into the sport by a strange twist of fate.

To anyone growing up in Canada, hockey is obviously the national sport. Boys and girls alike spend countless hours out in the cold honing their hockey skills with the hope of one day making it to the big time. Cindy Klassen was like most other girls involved in hockey during the late 1990s and wanted to join the Canadian national hockey team for the 1998 Olympics. Disappointed at not making the hockey team, and with her career prospects going nowhere, Klassen decided to try her hand at speed skating. She discovered quickly that she had a natural talent for the sport.

Four years after giving up her dreams of playing hockey for Canada, Klassen got to represent Canada in speed skating at the 2002 Winter Games in Salt Lake City and brought home her first Olympic medal, a bronze in the 3000 metres.

In between Olympic Games, Klassen distinguished herself as one of the top speed skating talents in the world by winning a host of other competitions. In November 2005 at the World Championships of speed skating, she achieved a new level of notoriety when she set a new world record in the 1500 metres in a time of 1:51.79 seconds, a time that still stands to this day and beats the old record by nearly one and a half seconds. From 2004 to 2007, she won 11 medals at the World Championships. But by far her biggest accomplishment came at the 2006 Olympics in Turin, Italy.

In a display of pure athleticism, Klassen took home five medals from those games: one gold, two silver and two bronze medals. Added to her bronze medal from the 2002 Games, she had won six medals, surpassing short track speed skater Marc Gagnon, track and field legend Phil Edwards, and multi-disciplined athlete cyclist and speed skater Clara Hughes, each of whom have five career Olympic medals.

One month after winning her sixth career medal in Turin, Klassen was back on the ice. At a competition in Calgary in March 2006, Klassen set two world records in the 1000 metres (1:13.11 seconds) and in the 3000 metres (3:53.34 seconds).

Klassen then decided to take a break from competitive skating to take care of her sister, who had received extensive injuries in a car accident. But there is no doubt that she will be among the hundreds of other proud Canadian athletes who will represent their country on home turf at the 2010 Winter Games in Vancouver.

Long Track Speed Skater
Jeremy Wotherspoon

At the World Championship, 33-year-old Saskatchewan native Jeremy Wotherspoon has won more medals than he has fingers to count them with, but at the Olympics, Wotherspoon has only one.

Jeremy Wotherspoon went into the 1998 Olympics in Nagano coming off a strong season on the World Cup circuit and posting impressive times in all his races. In the 500-metre event, he was up against some strong talent from Norway, Germany and Japan, but Wotherspoon managed to come in second and win the silver medal. The initial success was followed by a host of medals at the World Championships, in the sprint, 500 metre and 1000 metre, and by the time the 2002 Salt Lake City Olympics came along, he was the clear favourite in the sprint and 500 metre categories. But fate was not so kind to him in these Olympics. Going into the 500-metre event, all Wotherspoon had to do was skate without making an error, and he would almost certainly win a medal. But a crash in the finals put him out of contention, and he left Salt Lake City without stepping on to the podium.

But a host of other victories followed, at the World Championships following the 2002 Games, and going into the 2006 Turin Olympics, Wotherspoon was again listed as one of the favourites. But the Olympics seemed to be an unbreakable factor in his life, and he finished the 500-metre event in ninth place and the 1000-metre event in 11th spot.

The Turin Games especially frustrated Wotherspoon, who wanted so badly to live up to everyone's expectations. The disappointing results had him questioning his career, and for the 2006–07 skating season, Wotherspoon took some time off to re-evaluate whether he wanted to continue in the sport.

Luckily for Canadian fans, he decided to return. "I never would have come back from a season off if I didn't think I could be as good as I ever was, if not better. It would be pretty frustrating to take a year off and come back and race at a lower speed or get less out of it than before," he told Canadian Press.

Everything was going great on his comeback trail until the 2008 Berlin World Cup, when he fell and broke his arm. "At the time I went to a hospital in Berlin, they said it was a clean break and would heal as well with or without surgery…. But when it was re-examined at home, they didn't think it looked as clean," Wotherspoon said. "It was in about six pieces, so they put a plate and screws in."

He had to undergo a long recovery, but he has managed to push through the initial pain, with his sights firmly set on participating in the 2010 Games before a home crowd. He knows that it will be a battle, but the journey is what keeps him going.

"In this sport, you're trying to find every way that you can to improve and part of being able to improve is, me as an athlete, looking at myself and thinking, what are my weaknesses, what can I be better at, accepting criticism to work on those things and I think that's a big part of communication on a team," said Wotherspoon.

Short Track Nation

Racing at top speeds around an oval measuring 111 metres, the sharp turns combined with razor-sharp skates make short track speed skating one of the most dangerous on the Olympic calendar, but also one of the most anticipated. Although the sport only debuted in the Olympics in 1988 as a demonstration sport, it has actually been around since the early 1900s. It remained a recreational sport until it was officially adopted by the International Skating Union in 1967. The first short track World Championships were held in 1981.

Ever since short track speed skating entered into the Winter Olympics at the 1992 Games in Albertville, France, Canada has been one of the top competing countries in the sport. Although South Korea holds the honour of having won the most races and medals, Canada has held its own when it comes to breaking world records.

In a sport traditionally dominated by Québec-born athletes, Michael Gilday of Yellowknife is quickly making a name for himself on the international scene and recently served notice to the world when he set the world record in the 1000-metre race at a meet in Calgary with a time of 1:23.815 seconds. Gilday will be looking to repeat that incredible performance on the world stage and making it to the 2010 Olympics in Vancouver.

Canada has also been dominant in the relay races, led by athletes from Québec. The record in the 5000-metre relay event belongs to Canadians Charles Hamelin, François-Louis Tremblay, Steve Robillard and Mathieu Turcotte who set the bar at 6:39.990 seconds in 2005.

Short track speed skating is a sport of hundredths of seconds, and the Canadian records in all the events are just a few off the world-record place, meaning that at any given moment, the records could fall, and a Canadian could be back on top of the world. For example, Mathieu Turcotte's Canadian record in the 1500 metres is 2:10.713 seconds while the record holder at the time of this writing was Hyun-Soo Ahn of South Korea at 2:10.639 seconds

With this history of winning, and a host of athletes ready to take over the reins, the future looks bright for Canadian short track speed skating.

True Calling: Sylvie Daigle

In the early stages of most sports, there is always an individual that history can point to as the first to truly become a master of the game. For Canadian speed skating, Sylvie Daigle is that seminal figure.

The youngest in a family of five daughters and one son, Sylvie was a born skater. Graced with a natural fluidity on the ice and an athletic predisposition, she was only nine years old when she first competed in the Québec Games. Although she had tried out on the short track, through most of her early career she was a dedicated long track skater. She earned some respect in her sport after winning gold in several distances at the 1979 Canada Games, but she fell short on the world stage at the 1980 Winter Games in Lake Placid, coming in 19th place in the 500-metre event. She tried her best in long track but never seemed able to keep pace with the other competitors.

After consulting with trainers and doctors, she found out that she had chronic weakness in the muscles in her calves. This was a devastating blow for an athlete whose sport is based on the power generated in the legs. The news forced her to abandon long track. The 400-metre oval of a long track race requires too much effort in the legs, but the 111-metre circuit of short track speed skating fit Daigle perfectly. She had only flirted with the sport in the past but now she dedicated herself to it full time.

Throughout the mid-1980s, Daigle improved her technique in a sport that some classified as roller derby on ice,
and by 1985 she had won several World Championship
titles. Her World Championship victories satisfied her
desire to be the best in her sport, but like all short
track skaters, she wanted full recognition of the event
at the Olympics. After several years of petitioning the
IOC, short track speed skating was finally added to
the 1988 Olympic calendar in Calgary, but only as
a demonstration sport. If the IOC had given the sport
full medal status that year, Canada would not have
hosted another Olympic Games without having won a
gold medal, because that year Daigle took home a gold
in the 1500-metre race (she also won a silver and two
bronze).

They were bittersweet victories for Daigle, not having
the official Olympic gold medal around her neck, but
she and her fellow short track athletes had attracted
enough fan support to show the IOC governing body
that their sport belonged in the big show. The excellent
reviews of short track paid off, and it was announced
a few years later that at the 1992 Winter Games in
Albertville, France, the sport would finally receive full
medal status.

With Albertville fast approaching, Daigle set her
sights on the podium. She knew that at the age of 30,
she might not get another chance at an individual gold
medal and that other skaters, such as fellow Canadian

Nathalie Lambert, were quickly making a name for themselves in the sport. Daigle approached each competition leading up to the Games with the same passion she would have if it were the Olympics. Although she lost a few races in between the 1992 and 1994 Olympics, she was considered one of the front-runners to take gold in the 500 metres and the 3000 metres, both her strongest events.

In November 1991, in a pre-Olympic event at the Albertville Ice Hall, she won the 500 metres over top-ranked skater Yahei Zhang of China. Daigle covered the course in 46.72 seconds and became the first woman to break the 47-second mark. "Sure, it felt good," said Daigle to reporters after the race. "But it was just a first step. I haven't won an Olympic medal yet."

Not since the days of Gaetan Boucher had Canadian speed skating had a reason to celebrate. At the 1992 Games in Albertville, Sylvie Daigle had a chance to regain that feeling of victory and pride that Boucher had established almost a decade earlier.

Entering the inaugural 500-metre event at the 1992 Olympics as the clear favourite, Daigle knew that the other skaters would be gunning to strip her of the title. Among her toughest competitors were Zhang of China and American skater Cathy Turner. The American skater was well known to the field of skaters not for her speed or technique but for her rough, physical style. Many critics of Turner's said she belonged in a roller derby rather than on the skating oval. Daigle knew of the American skater's reputation and tried to stay clear of her during the opening stage of the race, but Turner managed to cut inside, making contact with Daigle's skate and sending her crashing to the ice. Looking up in disgust as the rest of the field made their way up the ice, Daigle glanced over at the referees, hoping to see some sign that they had seen the violation, but no call was made. In one single stride, American Cathy Turner had wiped out Canada's hope for a gold medal in the event. It was a devastating end to the one race in which Daigle felt she had the best chance to win gold. The loss burned deep, but Daigle got another chance at gold in the 3000-metre relay.

Daigle, skating with Nathalie Lambert, Annie Perreault and Angela Cutrone, was among the Canadian favourites to pull through the opening rounds and finish first in the finals. Although Cutrone and Perreault were solid skaters, Lambert and Daigle had the technique and power to challenge for the gold medal—without those two, Canada's medal chances dropped. But with Daigle anchoring the squad, the team made it to the finals with relative ease. The biggest challenge would be getting through the final race without getting tripped up by Cathy Turner. As it turned out, Daigle skated her leg of the race against Turner and was not about to make the same mistake twice. Heading into the corner with the dangerous Turner, Daigle sped by the American and never looked back. Holding on to the lead, the Canadians captured the win, and Daigle finally had her first Olympic gold.

"It was my last chance. It was the perfect end to our dream," said Daigle after the race.

Immediately following the Albertville Games, she retired from competitive racing to start a medical degree at the Université de Montréal, but after a year out of competition and with the 1994 Lillehammer Games drawing nearer, she suspended her studies and resumed training. She needed to prove to herself that she could do it. The Albertville Games had left behind a bad taste in her mouth because she wasn't able to prove that she could win an individual race, and she hoped Lillehammer would be different.

"I feel like there's unfinished business," Daigle said before racing in Lillehammer. "I prepared myself for Albertville, and I wanted to be satisfied with my performance. So I was really disappointed, frustrated and sad. I didn't accomplish what I set out to do."

Competing in the 3000-metre relay again was Nathalie Lambert, as well as Isabelle Charest and Christine Boudrias, and Daigle had a decent chance of adding another Olympic gold medal to her collection. Opening strong against the Americans, the Chinese and the South Koreans, the four Canadian women looked incredibly strong with each hand-off. But being a sport in which competitors race around a small oval at top speeds all trying to lay claim to a piece of the ice, sometimes accidents happen.

Christine Boudrias took a corner too fast, lost an edge and flew off into the padded boards. She had managed to tag the next Canadian skater, but Canada was now too far out to go for the gold medal. Making up for lost time, however, the Canadian women skated to a third-place finish, which was good enough for a bronze medal. South Korea got the gold and China the silver. Boudrias felt the complete weight of her fall as she and her teammates were about to ascend the podium to collect their bronze medal. But as she wiped the tears from her eyes, she saw the judges huddled in a corner. Something had changed.

The judges suddenly announced that the Chinese had been disqualified for interference. This meant Canada would get the silver. It wasn't the gold that Daigle had hoped for, but it was better than bronze. A few days after winning the silver in the 3000-metre relay, Daigle tried to get her individual gold in the 500-metre race but was taken out of contention in the quarter-finals when she collided with Russian skater Marina Pylaeva. It was a disappointing end to her Olympic career, but Daigle had so many other fond memories and championships to look back on.

After the 1994 Lillehammer Games, she returned to Montréal to finish her medical degree, which she completed in 1998.

Master Marc Gagnon

No other Canadian has dominated one sport the way Marc Gagnon has in speed skating. Since the sport began to achieve international recognition when it was added as a demonstration sport to the 1988 Winter Games in Calgary, the South Koreans basically had a monopoly on the podium. But with time, a new crop of Canadian athletes began to make a name for themselves and slowly crept onto those long-held Korean podiums. To be more precise, it was not all of Canada that began the drive to short track success; it was Québec.

In Québec, after the success of Gaetan Boucher, young athletes were instantly drawn to the sport when they saw one of their own bring home two gold medals at the 1984 Olympics. Although he was a long track skater, Boucher had shown that Canadians, and Québecers more specifically, could succeed on the world stage. His influence was so strong that Québec now boasts the highest number of short track speed skating clubs in Canada and has a history of excellent teaching and coaching that has produced Canada's best in the sport, Marc Gagnon being one of them.

First bursting onto the international stage at the 1993 World Short Track Championships in Beijing, a then 18-year-old Marc Gagnon made an instant impression on the competition when he won two gold medals, one silver and one bronze. With such impressive performances coming out of the World Championships, he was expected to do great things at the 1994 Olympics in Lillehammer, Norway, especially at the 1000-metre distance, which he had won easily at the World's.

Gagnon easily made it through the opening elimination rounds of the 1000-metre race and into the semifinals. As world champion of the event, he knew what he had to do to win the race, but he was also acutely aware of how quickly things could change in his sport. He would need to finish in the top two in the race to advance into the finals. From the opening signal Gagnon played the game with the other athletes, exchanging the lead several times in the first 500 metres before the pace began to pick up. Taking the early lead, he wanted to set the pace to his liking, but in a split second, he stumbled on a lane marker and fell crashing to the ice. In an instant he was out of the race and out of medal contention. Gagnon's consolation prize was the winning of the B-final.

Another Canadian, Derrick Campbell, made it into the finals, but he too ended up crashing. Only this time, Campbell was able to get up and finish the race in third place. Campbell was happy to get a medal but could only wonder how he might have done had it not been for the crash. But his bronze medal celebrations did not last long. The judges announced that Campbell had skated off the ice before he reached the finish line. This was an automatic disqualification, meaning that the bronze medal would go to the B-final winner, who was none other than Marc Gagnon.

Between the 1994 Winter Games in Lillehammer and the 1998 Games in Nagano, Gagnon kept adding to his trophy case, winning more medals at the World Championships. Having him on the speed skating scene meant that it was no longer the Koreans who owned the sport—Canada was now a major player, and Gagnon was the men's leader. In Nagano, he failed to take any individual gold medals but won a team gold in the 5000-metre relay. Again, he followed his performance at the 1998 Olympics with more medals at the World Championships until he arrived for his last and greatest performance of his career, at the 2002 Olympics.

The 2002 Olympic Games in Salt Lake City would be the 27-year-old's last shot at glory. It wasn't as if he needed it though, because, after 10 years of competition on the international stage, Gagnon had won a grand total of 35 medals at the World Championships alone. Another medal or two at the 2002 Olympics would simply be the icing on a great career. It was Gagnon's relaxed attitude that allowed him to approach the races in a new light, giving him more confidence in his abilities when it came time to race. After all, he had seen everything there was to see on the ice; all he had to do was skate the perfect race. The only thing he wanted to prove to himself was that he could win a single individual race.

Gagnon achieved that and more, winning a gold in the 500-metre sprint, another gold in the 5000-metre relay and a bronze in the 1500 metres. This brought his total medal count at all Olympics to five. It was the most any Canadian Winter Olympian had ever won in history. (Cindy Klassen later beat the record, winning six medals in total.) After the 2002 Olympic Games, Gagnon retired from competitive skating. For his incredible accomplishments, he was inducted into the Canadian Sports Hall of Fame in 2008.

2010 Olympic Long Track Speed Skating Schedule

Location: Richmond, BC
Medal Ceremonies: BC Place Stadium

Richmond Olympic Oval (capacity: 8000)

February 13: Men's 5000 metre
February 14: Women's 3000 metre
February 15: Men's 500 metre
February 16: Women's 500 metre
February 17: Men's 1000 metre
February 18: Women's 1000 metre
February 20: Men's 1500 metre
February 21: Women's 1500 metre
February 23: Men's 10,000 metre
February 24: Women's 5000 metre

February 26: Men's and Women's team pursuit,
    qualifying
February 27: Men's and Women's team pursuit,
    finals

2010 Olympic Short Track Speed Skating Schedule

Location: Vancouver, BC
Medal Ceremonies: BC Place Stadium

Pacific Coliseum, Hastings Park (capacity: 14,239)

February 13: Women's 500 metre, qualifying
February 13: Women's 3000-metre relay, qualifying
February 13: Men's 1500 metre
February 17: Men's 1000 metre, qualifying
February 17: Men's 5000-metre relay, qualifying
February 17: Women's 500 metre, finals
February 20: Women's 1500 metre
February 20: Men's 1000 metre, finals
February 24: Women's 1000 metre, qualifying
February 24: Men's 500 metre, qualifying
February 24: Women's 3000-metre relay, finals
February 26: Men's 500 metre, finals
February 26: Women's 1000 metre, finals
February 26: Men's 5000-metre relay, finals

Chapter Six

Snow Sports

Canada is perceived as a land of ice and snow, but this intimate access to the cold has not always translated into success in snow sports. From the very first Olympic Winter Games, Canada excelled in one sport, hockey. Except for a few medals in speed skating at the 1932 Lake Placid Games (a statistical anomaly since most European competitors did not make the transatlantic crossing to participate; Canada and the U.S. dominated those games), in the first three Olympics, all Canada won were hockey medals.

An Olympic medallist in skiing did not surface until the 1956 Games when Lucie Wheeler won a bronze medal in the women's downhill. Canada did not produce a gold medallist until Anne Heggtveit won the slalom in 1960. Canadian men were a lot slower coming out of the blocks, winning their first medal in 1980 when Steve Podborski won a bronze in downhill. Although Canada has never dominated the podium on the slopes, some shining moments have made sports history.

Record Gold: Anne Heggtveit

Not many world-class downhill skiers come out of the Ottawa region. With few mountains close by, many of which would be classified as "hills" by European standards, eastern Canada never really produced any major alpine skiers. That is, until the arrival of Anne Heggtveit.

Her ascension to the crown of Canadian world-class skier was made a little easier by being born into a skiing family. Her Norwegian-born father was the 1934 Canadian cross-country skiing champion, and Anne also had two uncles who represented Canada at the 1932 and 1936 Olympics. Although she enjoyed cross-country skiing, the thrill and excitement of downhill skiing made the sport impossible to resist. By the age of 13 she had already won all the local cross-country competitions several times over and was in need of a new challenge.

At 15, Heggtveit made the leap onto the international stage in 1954 in an appearance at Norway's Holmenkollen. Competing in the giant slalom, Heggtveit stunned her older and more seasoned competition by coming away with a first-place finish. No one gave the young girl from the flat capital of Canada any hopes of winning, but when she was done carving up the Norwegian mountains, every competitor surely remembered her name.

Because of Anne's impressive wins at such an early age, the Canadian ski team added her to the roster for the 1956 Winter Games in Cortina d'Ampezzo, Italy.

Competing in the downhill event, Heggtveit was no match for the top skiers in the world and finished in 22nd spot. She hadn't gone into the Olympics with any particular goals in mind. She knew at just 17 years old that she still had a lot to learn on her skis and that the Olympics was a way to get her accustomed to competing against the best in the world.

Returning home with her lesson learned, Heggtveit focused on her training and set her sights on winning gold at the 1960 Olympics. But just as her career started to move in a positive direction, she suffered a series of injuries that took her out of competition for much of the late 1950s. It was a difficult time for the young skier, but by 1959 she was back in competitive form and was racing across North America and Europe. It seemed as though the time off the mountain was a good thing.

Heggtveit won her first major European competition in St. Moritz, Switzerland, placing first in the slalom event and first in the alpine combined. She later followed that up with first-place finishes in the downhill and slalom at the Canadian National Championships. By the time the 1960 Squaw Valley Winter Olympics in California rolled around, she was one of the favourites to take home at least one medal in the alpine events. But she was taking nothing for granted.

Going into the Olympics with a renewed sense of hope after her comeback from injury and her recent performances in international competition, Heggtveit was looking to make her mark early in the Games with her favourite events, the downhill and giant slalom. But the 21-year-old had to settle for a 12th-place finish in both events.

Canada was not having the greatest Olympics up to that point. Of the 44 team members sent to the Games, only pairs figure skaters Barbara Wagner and Bob Paul had won a gold medal, and the Canadian men's hockey team had lost a pivotal game to the United States. Despite the morose feeling among the Canadian camp, Heggtveit felt good when she hit the slopes on February 26 for her last shot at gold in the slalom event.

Standing at the top of Papoose Mountain before the first of her two runs, Heggtveit looked over to her coach and something inside herself told her that it was going to be a good day. "I've got a feeling this is it," she said to her coach.

Heggtveit would run second to French skier Therese Leduc. It was a good position for the Canadian skier as she was able to judge the relative speed of the course and the time she would need to finish. Leduc ran the course in a respectable 59.2 seconds. Next up was Heggtveit.

She perched herself on the edge of the mountain and launched herself down toward the finish line; it was all or nothing. Keeping focused as she sped down the mountain, she tore through the 50 gates. Apart from a slight stumble at the 10th gate, she blazed through the course in an incredible 54 seconds flat. The crowd cheered the Canadian on, realizing that they had just witnessed something special. One by one the best skiers in the world passed through those same 50 gates, but none could match Heggtveit's time. The closest was the 15th skier, Marianne Jahn of Austria, who finished the run in 55.5 seconds.

Barring a complete disaster in the second run, Heggtveit had all but wrapped up the gold medal. She had to decide whether to ski the course conservatively to safeguard her spot or to blaze down the hill like she did in the first run and assure her spot at the top of the podium.

"I used to have a bad habit of holding back in my second run," she later recalled, "but this time I didn't hold back at all. I knew that the other girls were good enough that I couldn't."

She attacked the course with the same ferocity and skill and was able to cross the line in 55.6 seconds. But again she had to wait as the rest of the field completed their second runs. As the name of each new skier was announced, she whispered to herself, "It's not finished yet." And as skier after skier crossed the line, it became obvious that Heggtveit had locked up the gold-medal position.

Only the last skier of the day could possibly challenge her for the top spot. Austrian skier Marianne Jahn completed her first run 1.5 seconds behind Heggtveit, but would need a miracle run of somewhere around a 53-second finish. It wasn't impossible but probably unlikely. Heggtveit watched as Jahn tore down the course, looking very much like she could finish in record time, but about a few hundred feet from the finish line, she stumbled and fell down. She managed to pull herself up and finish the race, but it was too late. Heggtveit won the race by an incredible combined total of 3.3 seconds over her closest rival.

Her father remarked in an interview after the race that the Canadian hockey team's loss to the Americans might have given her the ammunition she needed to win the gold for Canada. "I think it might have been the inspiration. It takes just some little things to get them steamed up. I think, knowing Anne, that it would be just the type of thing that would make her grit her teeth a little harder."

Her slalom win not only established the record for the largest margin of victory in an alpine event but also garnered the first Canadian gold medal in skiing at the Winter Games. Wanting to go out on top, after the closing ceremony, Anne Heggtveit retired from competitive skiing. Upon retirement she was inducted into the Canadian Sports Hall of Fame.

Nancy "Tiger" Greene

Although she retired from competitive downhill skiing at the age of 24, Nancy Greene left a lasting impression on Canadian athletics and a legacy that lasts until today. Dubbed Canada's tiger of the slopes because of her fearless approach, Greene didn't achieve instant success on the world stage.

Raised at the foot of the Canadian Rockies, Nancy Greene first hit the slopes at the age of three. Both her parents were avid weekend skiers and often took their daughter with them. Nancy proved to be a quick study and in no time skied circles around her parents. Skiing, however, remained a leisurely pursuit for Greene until fate stepped in when, at the age of 14, she got the chance to test her skills against other girls her age.

In 1958, young skiers from across Canada descended on her hometown of Rossland, BC, to compete in the Canadian junior championships. It just so happened that two girls from the British Columbia team had been injured on one of the steep practice slopes. The BC coach, who already had Nancy's older sister on the team, knew about the younger Greene's ability on the slopes and asked her to be part of the team. Half a day later she was booming down the hill and finished the slalom in third place. The thrill of the competition sparked something inside the young Greene and soon she was entering every race she could. She devoted herself to a strict training regimen, and 18 months later she was invited to join the Canadian Olympic program. At just 16 years old, she made her first appearance at the Olympics in 1960 at Squaw Valley.

She did not end up winning any medals, finishing well back in both the slalom and giant slalom, but it was a valuable experience for such a young athlete, made even more so because she got to share a room with Anne Heggtveit, who went on to win gold in the slalom event.

Once the Olympics were over, Greene went right back out into competition, but in her final race in the winter of 1961, she took a horrible tumble and broke her leg. It was an injury that changed her career for the better. During her recovery, her coach put her on a weight training program, a system that lay the eventual groundwork for her future successes. The weights not only helped her recover from her injuries, but they also strengthened her legs, which allowed her to attack the slopes like she had never done before. With a new confidence and a completely healed leg, Greene returned to the slopes and was set to make her mark at the 1964 Olympics in Innsbruck.

She now had the strength and some experience behind her to compete with the best in the world, but she still lacked the technical qualities for which she would become known. She finished a disappointing seventh in the downhill, 16th in the slalom and 15th in the giant slalom. It was a huge disappointment for Greene, but she was not about to give up. She doubled her training efforts on and off the slopes and, finally, in 1965 it began to pay dividends. At the U.S. Nationals, Greene surprised with first-place finishes in both slalom and giant slalom and a fourth-place finish in the downhill.

Just a year later, she was dominating the World Cup circuit and getting the recognition she deserved. Her skiing style was hard and aggressive, and although she took a few tumbles along the way, Greene had carved out a place as the best in the world. It was with this momentum that she approached the 1968 Olympics in Grenoble, France.

But just a few weeks before the Games, Greene injured her ankle in training. She kept off her skis for the two weeks prior to the start of the Games and was still considered the medal favourite, if, of course, she recovered from her injuries. By the time of the opening ceremony, Greene's ankle had completely healed, and she proudly walked ahead of her fellow athletes as Canada's flag bearer.

But as much as the honour of carrying her nation's flag meant to her, nothing was more important than winning on the slopes, and the one race she wanted to win was the downhill. She had already proven to herself on the World Cup circuit that she could win in the slalom events, but a decisive downhill victory still eluded her.

But Greene's chance at the downhill podium was not to be. Apparently some dirt had been tracked across the slope and had gotten stuck to the bottom of her skis, which slowed her down enough to put her out of medal contention. At the bottom of the hill, she was almost in tears when the Canadian media interviewed her. It was a tough loss, but it made her all the more determined to succeed in the slalom events.

In the slalom, she was just 0.2 seconds behind the winner, Mareille Goitschell of France, which was good enough for the silver medal. In the giant slalom, Greene dominated the field completely, finally getting her hands on that Olympic gold medal she had always wanted. The slopes were icy and well worn, but her weight training had paid off, enabling her to stick to the snow on the curves and power down the hill.

After the Olympics, Greene went on to clinch her second World Cup in giant slalom, and just a few months before her 25th birthday she was named the best overall Canadian Athlete of the Year and Canada's Woman of the Year. Endorsement deals and speaking engagements flooded in, and soon everyone in Canada knew about Nancy Greene. But with no more areas in skiing left to conquer, shortly after her birthday she announced that she was retiring from competitive skiing.

But Greene did not stay away from the sport for long. She and her husband Al Raine were instrumental in the early development of the Whistler-Blackcomb Resort area in British Columbia, and they established the Nancy Greene Ski League that has helped young Canadian athletes wanting to get a start on the slopes.

For her achievements both on and off the slopes, the Canadian Press named her Canada's Female Athlete of the Century. Most recently she was named as a permanent member of the Canadian Senate.

Kerrin Lee-Gartner

From the town of Trail, BC, Kerrin Lee-Gartner was surrounded by mountains as a child and had an easy time getting to know the sport of downhill skiing. Growing up during the time of the "Crazy Canucks," young Kerrin used the inspiration of those intrepid Canadian skiers to pursue a path of her own. The Crazy Canucks were a group of alpine skiers who rose to prominence in the 1970s. The reputation of Dave Irwin, Dave Murray, Steve Podborski and Ken Read for fast and seemingly reckless skiing earned them the name of Crazy Canucks.

Beginning her amateur career with the Canadian Women's Ski Team in 1982, Lee-Gartner did not get off to an easy start. For many years she was hampered by numerous knee injuries and was forced to have several operations over the years so that she could continue pursuing her sport. Each injury was a crushing blow that made her question her belief that this was the right path for her, yet every time she hit the slopes, her passion for the sport was reignited.

For Lee-Gartner, the 1990s were a far better decade for her career. Slowly, she began showing what she could do on the national and international circuits with a string of top-10 placements. It was the perfect time for her to begin to peak as the 1992 Olympics in Albertville were fast approaching.

As well as she was doing, the situation in the Canadian national ski program was falling apart. Ken Read, one of the original Crazy Canucks during the '70s and '80s, described the performance of the team in the international competitions as an embarrassment and not something that Canada had ever been known for. At the 1992 Alpine Skiing World Cup, the Canadian men's team failed to register any sort of competitive challenge and consistently finished out of the top 10, sometimes even failing to qualify for certain races. The women fared slightly better, with only Kerrin Lee-Gartner managing a fourth-place finish in the downhill results.

At the Albertville Games, things went from bad to worse for Team Canada. The men's best hope, Ed Podivinsky, was injured when he caught an edge on one of his runs and crashed. Cary Mullen, Brian Stemmle and Rob Crossan were taken out of medal contention when they wiped out on their respective runs. It was an utter disaster for Canadian skiing. The women did not do any better as many of them were out with injuries. That left only Kerrin Lee-Gartner and Michelle McKendry.

Sports analysts did not give Lee-Gartner or McKendry much hope of defeating the likes of such skiing greats as German Katja Seizinger, Austrian Petra Kronberger and American Hilary Lindh. These athletes had made a name for themselves on the World

Cup circuit, and each went on to have incredible careers. Lee-Gartner had never won a World Cup race, and her injuries always seemed to play a factor in her results. However, when she posted the third fastest time in the practice run, it signalled to the other racers that she had arrived and was ready to complete, though few television and radio commentators paid much attention to her results. Practice was one thing, going for the gold was an entirely new race, and practices no longer mattered.

The race was held on February 15 on a hill called "Roc de Fer" (Iron Rock), one of the toughest courses in women's downhill history. Steep, icy and having terrifying jumps, the hill had claimed many of Lee-Gartner's teammates earlier in the week. The skiers even gave one of the jumps a nickname. They called it "Noodles," because that's what the skier looked like after jumping off it. Many skiers, in fact, slowed down on purpose when approaching the jump, claiming it was downright suicidal.

Lee-Gartner, however, was not afraid; she was, after all, a Crazy Canuck. "The approach I took was all or nothing," she said. "I was going after the podium no matter what!" It was the sort of attitude she would need to defeat such great skiers and defy the killer course.

Racing 12th out of 34 skiers, Lee-Gartner had already watched Seizinger and Kronberger shoot the course, so she knew what time she had to beat to have a chance at the podium. She hit the top of the course bombing down without a second thought to her safety, hitting speeds of over 100 kilometres per hour. At every timing interval on the upper portion of the course, Lee-Gartner posted the second-best split times behind Seizinger. But it was on the bottom of the course that she truly poured on the magic.

Sailing over the Noodle jump with ease, she zoomed across the finish line 0.12 seconds ahead of Seizinger. As she cheered in delight, the crowd of some 10,000 spectators looked on in disbelief as this previously unknown Canadian suddenly stole the spotlight and possibly the gold medal. Now came the hardest part. She had to wait while 19 other skiers tried their best to beat her time.

Two skiers came within seconds of beating her time but were not close enough. Lee-Gartner had won her and the country's first Olympic gold medal in down-hill racing. Not even the Crazy Canucks had achieved her level of success. Following the Olympics, she continued to ski for another few years before retiring from competitive skiing in 1994 after the World Cup. She continues to stay close to the sport as a commentator for Canadian television.

Alpine Skier Erik Guay

Missing out on a bronze medal in the super-G at the 2006 Olympic Games in Turin by 0.1 seconds was a tough pill to swallow for Erik Guay, but he has never backed down from a challenge, and in the years since the heartbreaking finish he has shown the world that there are still a few Crazy Canucks left.

Although born in the metropolis of Montréal, Guay's true home has been two hours outside of the city on the slopes of Mont-Tremblant. It was on those slopes that he honed his craft and began moving up in the ski world. Owning the slopes in Canada was something that came at an early age, but true accomplishment in alpine skiing comes from winning in front of a global audience.

In 2000, Guay made the jump into World Cup competition. His first few years on the World Cup circuit were not all that successful, but he was adding to his bank of experiences and setting himself up for success in the future. In 2003, all the hard work finally began to pay off. In November of that year he captured his first World Cup podium finish with a downhill silver medal in Lake Louise. But just one month after experiencing the high point of his career, he suffered the worst injury imaginable for a career skier. At a World Cup event in Gardena, Italy, Guay crashed into the compression fence on the side of the slope and completely tore the anterior cruciate ligament in his left knee. Looking back on the crash, Guay said, "I got close to 90 to 100 metres of air before I crashed into the compression." It would take a year before he was back on his skis again and competing at the level that he was accustomed to.

In the lead up to the 2006 Olympics, Guay reached the World Cup podium three times, establishing himself as a legitimate competitor for a medal. But just two weeks before the opening ceremonies, he suffered another injury that threatened to take him out of the Olympics. He injured that same left knee during a training run. But he never gave up on his dream of competing for his country at the Olympics.

In order to give his knee enough time to heal, he voluntarily removed himself from the downhill and giant slalom to focus solely on his best event, the super-G. When the event got underway, Guay had barely spent any time on his skis since his injury. Yet despite the problems, he finished the run in 1:30.98—good enough for third place with just three skiers left in the race. The next two skiers failed to beat his time, but the final skier, Austria's Herman Maier, beat Guay out by 0.3 seconds. Maier's time placed him in second and bumped Guay down to fourth, missing a bronze by 0.1 seconds.

Rather than viewing the Olympic result as a defeat, Guay used his motivation on the slopes to propel him to higher levels on the World Cup circuit. Going into the 2010 Games in Vancouver, he now has the experience and training necessary to win gold before a home crowd. All he has to do is stay healthy.

Alpine Skier Emily Brydon

Thirty-year-old Emily Brydon of Fernie, BC, got her start on the international skiing stage in 1998 when she made her first World Cup appearance, and by 2000 she had achieved her first podium finish at the age of 20 in the World Downhill in Switzerland. The Canadian national ski team had high hopes for Brydon, given her young age and already stand-out performances, but those highs were followed by a literal crashing low when she tore the ligament in her right knee at the start of the season in 2001. Six months later, she crashed on a training run, tearing the ligament in her left knee. Her participation at the 2002 Olympics in Salt Lake City, Utah, looked to be in jeopardy if she could not rehabilitate both knees in time.

With hard work and painful sessions with her personal trainer, Brydon was able to make it to her first Olympics, but the result of two newly healed knees on the slopes was more cautious runs in competition and therefore a slower time. She finished the slalom event in 27th place and 38th in the giant slalom. Brydon described her Olympic debut as a "bittersweet experience." It was nice for her to come back from injury and get to go to the Olympics, but she was not in 100 percent physical and mental shape and finished well out of the top spots.

A series of World Cup victories from 2003 to 2005 placed Brydon as one of the better skiers in the World and therefore higher expectations were on her when it came time for the 2006 Olympics.

She improved in her second Olympics in 2006 in Italy, finishing ninth in super-G, 13th in the combined and 20th in the downhill. The results were better than her first Olympics, but it left her questioning her future in competitive skiing. Fortunately for Canadian skiing, she knew her career wasn't over yet.

A couple of years ago after the (2002) Olympics I really thought about retiring, but I realized I hadn't achieved all the goals I had set out, not that you're going to achieve all of them, but I didn't think that I had given it enough of a shot yet. As an athlete you never want to leave the sport with regrets.

Brydon now has her sights set on the 2010 Games in Vancouver, which will most likely be her final Olympics.

Biathlete Myriam Bedard

Canadians already knew Myriam Bedard's name from her 1992 Albertville Olympic bronze medal victory in the women's 15-kilometre biathlon. But it was at the 1994 Games in Lillehammer, Norway, that the world was introduced to the beautiful Canadian from Neufchatel, Québec.

Bedard was a natural fit for the sport of biathlon, which is a combination of cross-country skiing and target shooting. Competitors ski at breakneck speeds between target areas, pull into the shooting station, get off the required number of shots and then ski to the finish line. Bedard had been a member of the Royal Canadian Army Cadets since the age of 14 and participated in her first biathlon when she was 15; she proved to have a knack for the sport. Her first love as a child was actually figure skating, but the expense of skates and renting ice time prohibited her from following that dream. In her teenage years, the biathlon had become her passion, and the training paid immediate dividends for the young athlete.

In her first competitive race, wearing a pair of rented skis and boots with tissue stuffed in the toes, she managed to beat all other competitors. Introverted and quiet, Bedard was drawn to the solitude of the biathlon. Hitting the trails alone, away from the noise and commotion of daily life, was her way of coping with stress and allowed her the time to think.

The poise and grace gained from the meditative time alone on the trails gave her the ability to block out distractions and enabled her to focus completely on winning a race. She was getting so good at her craft that in 1987, at 18 years of age, she won the Canadian Junior Championship.

In 1991, she became only the second Canadian to win a World Cup biathlon event, and as a result, was invited to join the Canadian team for the 1992 Winter Olympics in Albertville, France. This would be the first time women competed in the biathlon event at the Olympics, and Bedard wanted to make her mark on the sport right from the start.

Competing in the 15-kilometre event in which the skier stops four times—twice to shoot five shots in the prone position, and twice to shoot standing—Bedard had an excellent race. She finished with one of the best times in the top 10, but missing two targets cost her the gold medal (one minute is added to a competitor's time for missing a shot). She settled for the bronze.

In 1993, she redeemed her performance with a gold-medal win at the World Championship in the 7.5-kilometre race and silver in the 15-kilometre. But it was the 1994 Olympics in Lillehammer, Norway, that she had set her sights on. Throughout the month leading up to the Games, she deliberately slacked off on her training and underperformed at the World Cup events. Her ultimate goal was to qualify for the Olympics. It was there that she intended to give all of herself, and a few days before her race she threw herself into a self-imposed exile. She ate her meals alone, did not talk to anyone and ran the course over and over again in her mind. The biathlon is a test of endurance and will, and she was willing herself into a zone.

On the day of the 15-kilometre race, Bedard's only thoughts were on skiing, and she was anxious to begin. All the waiting was getting on her nerves and, being a crowd favourite, she had to deal with the constant attention from her fans. "What I found hardest," she said after the race, "was everything going on around me. People were yelling, 'Go, Myriam, Go,' and I was becoming distracted. I had to regain the mental state I'd put myself in over the last five days."

Because she started 67th out of 70 athletes, Bedard got a sense of how the competition was doing, and she was able to pass many of the other competitors during the race. She maintained an incredible pace throughout the entire 15-kilometre course, and in the shooting portion of the event she was steady and accurate, missing only two of 20 shots. Her closest rival, France's Anne Briand, missed three shots in the competition, and when Bedard crossed the line she was 46 seconds ahead of the French athlete. No other competitor came close to Bedard's time, and when she crossed the finish she knew she had just had the race of her career.

A few hours after the event, Bedard stood on a stage in downtown Lillehammer and watched as the Canadian flag was raised on the highest flagpole and the band blared out the first notes of "O Canada." With a huge grin plastered on her face, she took in every second of the triumphant moment. But always the serious competitor, Bedard was already thinking about the next race.

"I will enjoy this tonight," she said, with the gold medal hanging from her neck. "But tomorrow I will be thinking about the 7.5-kilometre race."

However, controversy surrounding the race win threatened to ruin her celebrations. One TV commentator noted that the targets used in the competition had not been functioning properly and that several shots taken by Bedard's opponents had failed to register as direct hits. The accusation was backed up by video footage that showed shadows appearing on the targets that the TV commentator had interpreted as direct hits. If it were true, the other athletes would have to be awarded the points, and Bedard might lose her gold medal.

Olympic officials immediately launched an investigation and discovered that the bullets had actually struck the perimeter of the targets and that upon shattering, one of the bullet fragments had hit the target, but the broken pieces did not have enough force to register as a hit. Her victory stood, and Bedard could now focus on her next challenge.

In the 15-kilometre race, Bedard had pretty much walked away with the gold medal after her dominant performance, but the 7.5-kilometre event was a different story. Her competition knew that she was the one to beat, and they chased her through the entire race. Bedard once again had the lucky draw of starting later in the race, so she had some idea of the time she needed to achieve the win.

Bedard had a good race, but throughout the course she noticed something odd about her skis. It wasn't until she missed two targets, for a time of 26:08.8, that she realized her skis had not been waxed properly. One ski was waxed for cold snow, the other for warmer conditions. All cross-country skiers know that proper waxing equals a smooth glide over the snow's surface, and for the Olympic athlete, proper waxing can take seconds off a race.

As Bedard entered the stadium for the end of the race, her time was very close to the Belarusian Svetlana Paramygina. The crowd of some 30,000 spectators looked back and forth between the clock and Bedard as she huffed her way to the finish line, crossing 1.1 seconds ahead of Paramygina and into first place. But Bedard could not start celebrating just yet. Her time was good, but Inna Sheshilki of Kazakstan burst into the stadium and looked to challenge for the gold. Bedard could only stand off to the side and watch her fate decided by her competitor.

Sheshilki burned through her last remaining reserves to reach the finish line, but just when it looked as though she had sealed the gold medal, her body shut down. Two metres from the finish line, she stumbled and fell to the ground. Meanwhile, the clock kept ticking away, and her hopes of a gold medal with it. Sheshilki managed to pick herself up and lunge across the finish line. The fall cost her dearly as she finished out of the medals in fourth place.

Myriam Bedard could now celebrate winning two gold medals in one Winter Olympics—the only other Canadian Olympian to have done that at that time was speed skater Gaetan Boucher.

Bedard had won, but after the race, she could not help but wonder about those mismatched skis. "When you consider it, I won the race by only 1.1 seconds. If I had not won, I would have thought about this the rest of my life."

Biathlon Hopes Zina Kocher and Jean Philippe Le Guellec

It has been more than a decade since Myriam Bedard brought the sport of biathlon to the attention of the Canadian population by winning double gold medals at the 1994 Winter Games in Lillehammer, Norway, and since that time Canadians have been hoping for one of their athletes to get back onto the podium.

The fact is that the Europeans dominate the sport of biathlon. The French, the Russians and the Scandinavian countries have literally owned the podium over the years, and any other nation had to consider itself lucky just to get close to the top three. Although Canada did have its moment in the sun in 1994, the road to gold has been dark ever since. But all hope is not lost.

Canada's best shot at Olympic glory in the biathlon rests in the capable and steady hands of Canmore, Alberta's Zina Kocher and Québec City's Jean Philippe Le Guellec. These two athletes will enter the 2010 Games as Olympic veterans, having both competed at the 2006 Turin Olympics. Neither athlete succeeded in getting near to the podium in 2006, but the experience of the event was something that will surely prepare them to compete against the world's best in front of a home crowd in 2010.

Jean Philippe's most recent results on the international stage show that he is ready to take his career to the next level. During the 2008–09 World Cup season he managed two top-10 finishes and placed 16th in the 2009 World Championship relay race.

Kocher has had slightly greater success on the world stage, placing third in the 2006 World Cup individual race and taking gold at the National Championships in 2007 and 2008 in the 10-kilometre pursuit and the 7.5-kilometre sprints.

All of Canada will be watching to see if one of them can make history.

Nearly Up in Smoke

The only people I could see being interested in him would be the Hemp Growers of America.

–Comment made by a New York management-consulting firm on Ross Rebagliati's chances of getting endorsement deals after testing positive for marijuana during the 1998 Winter Olympics

Ross Rebagliati was just another snowboarder trying to make his mark on the sport. So when the International Olympic Committee (IOC) decided to make snowboarding a medal event for the 1998 Winter Olympics in Nagano, Japan, Rebagliati seized the opportunity to grab a piece of the spotlight.

His event was the snowboarding giant slalom, and after several runs Rebagliati was at the top of the standings poised to take home a medal—it just remained to be seen what colour it would be. On February 8, 1998, Rebagliati tore down the course in his final run and won snowboarding gold for Canada. It was an amazing finish for the 26-year-old Canadian rider, and his hometown of Whistler, BC, went wild, celebrating his golden victory.

The celebrations, however, were short lived. Two days after his gold-medal performance on the hills of Shiga Kogen, Rebagliati tested positive for an illegal substance. It wasn't the performance-enhancing drug that Ben Johnson had tested positive for during the 1988 Summer Olympics, it wasn't a drug that would make his reaction time faster or his muscles larger—the drug found in Ross Rebagliati's system was marijuana.

Rebagliati never admitted to having smoked marijuana in the months prior to the Olympics, and the only reason he could think of why trace amounts of the drug were in his system was that a few nights before leaving for the Olympics, he had attended a party where several people were smoking the drug. Regardless of the circumstances, he was stripped of his medal, to which the Canadian Olympic Committee immediately responded with an appeal to reverse the decision. Rebagliati was devastated.

"All I had in my head was Ben Johnson and how everyone hated him," he told *Maclean's* magazine. "I was ready to fly straight from Japan right to South America. I wasn't even going to come home, I was thinking, for years."

On Rebagliati's side of this international mess was that marijuana wasn't considered a performance-enhancing drug; in fact, it had the opposite effect. Had he truly smoked marijuana before the race, his gold medal would have been all the more impressive. Although the media had treated Ben Johnson's steroid use as the saddest moment in Canada's sporting history, Rebagliati's pot bust was considered a joke, with the blond Canadian's smoking-fast run used as the punchline.

For Rebagliati, the controversy was all a little too surreal. "I've been training for 11 years to be the best snowboarder in the world, and that goal was achieved on February 8 in Shiga Kogen," he told the press at a news conference before Canada appealed to the International Olympic Committee. "I've worked too hard to let it slip through my fingers. I am in favour of this decision to appeal the IOC executive board's decision and will be working with the COA to prepare that appeal."

After all the media attention and public scrutiny, the IOC decided to return Rebagliati's gold medal and allow him to return home an Olympic hero. Thanks to Ross Rebagliati, snowboarding's introduction to the world at the Nagano Olympics was anything but quiet, and snowboarding managed to retain its image as an outsider sport whose participants don't play by the normal rules.

Snowboard Sensation Jasey-Jay Anderson

The senior member of the Canadian snowboard team, Montréal-born Jasey-Jay Anderson has been shredding up mountains across Canada and around the world for well over a decade. He is Canada's most decorated snowboarder, but there is still one title he has not added to his list: Olympic medallist. Now entering his mid-30s, Anderson's last chance to prove he can win at all levels will take place in Vancouver. He has had three tries at making the podium, but none would be more special than to win in front of fellow Canadian citizens.

The importance of the Vancouver Games has not been lost on the veteran. "This year, I actually told myself I have to focus on snowboarding," he says. "It's my last year as a full-time athlete. So this summer will be super intense for physical workouts. You have to maximize everything because it's pre-Olympics, man—you've got to be on it. Whatever I've been kind [of] putting off for the last couple of years, I can't this year."

At Anderson's first Olympics in 1998, he seemed poised to win the gold medal after his first run, finishing in first place. However, by the time he was ready to take his second and final run for a medal, heavy fog had rolled in and limited visibility. The conditions greatly affected his run and dropped him down to 16th place. His teammate Ross Rebagliati took home the gold medal.

Anderson returned to the Olympics in 2002 with something to prove. He had already shown the world and himself that he could win on the World Cup circuit against the best athletes, but for some reason the Olympics seemed cursed. He failed to qualify for the elimination heats in the parallel giant slalom and ended up in 29th position overall. After the 2002 Games, Anderson nearly quit the sport, but the call of the mountain was too strong, and he was soon back to form, winning races on the World Cup circuit.

At the 2006 Games in Turin, things got a little better for Anderson in the new event of snowboard cross, where he finished in fifth place, but his bread-and-butter event, the parallel giant slalom, ended in another disaster when he came in 20th overall. Trying to find the reason for the continuing disappointment at the Olympics was getting tough, and again Anderson questioned whether he had the energy to wait for another Olympics. But when it was announced that a Canadian city would be hosting the 2010 Games, Anderson knew that he had to try one more time. He is hoping that his first-place finish in the parallel giant slalom in January 2009 will be a harbinger of good things to come.

The Québec Air Force

At the 1994 Games in Lillehammer, the sport of free-style ski jumping made its debut as a full medal sport. Canadians had already distinguished themselves in this daring sport in which athletes launch down a steep embankment toward a near vertical jump, where they perform a series of twists and turns in the air before, hopefully, landing back on their skis. At the 1992 Albertville Games, freestyle ski aerials was a demonstration sport, and Canada's own Philippe Laroche took home the gold medal. Canadians had high hopes for their athletes by the time the 1994 Games rolled around.

Under the coaching of Yves Laroche (brother of Philippe), the hub of aerial athletes for Canada were all from Québec. The 1994 aerial team consisted of Philippe Laroche, Lloyd Langlois, Nicolas Fontaine and Andy Capicik—better known as the "Québec Air Force." The team had dominated on the world stage leading up to the Olympics and was expected to be leaders in Lillehammer. Head coach Yves Laroche had a lot to be proud of when his entire team qualified for the final medal round of the event.

After the Canadians' performances in the qualifying round, they were expected to walk away with the gold, but no one had really counted on Swiss aerialist Andreas Schonbachler. The veteran athlete had announced before the start of the Games that it would be his last competition, and he saved his best for his final jump. He hit the ramp perfectly, twisting and turning in the air without any flaws, and landed with ease. He knew he had made a great jump, and the crowd knew it too.

After watching Schonbachler's jump, the Québec Air Force realized they would have to pull off something special to beat him. Lloyd Langlois was first up for the Canadians. He hit the ramp perfectly, pulled off his triple-twisting triple (that is, three twists and three somersaults in the air) and landed with ease, but the judges gave him lower scores than the Swiss.

The other Canadians could not match Schonlachler's performance, but they still had one last hope, Philippe Laroche. If anyone could beat Schonbachler, it was Laroche. He raced down the hill, soared off the jump and did one of the most difficult twists and turns in the sport, technically called a full-full-full. The only flaw with his routine was on the landing. Laroche managed to stay upright, but it was a little rough in execution. The judges' scores reflected that slight error and placed Laroche in second place. It was a silver for Laroche and a bronze for Langlois. It was a tough result for the Canadians to swallow, but Schonbachler deserved the gold.

Aside from losing the gold, the Québec Air Force owned the top six positions. Andy Capicik finished in fourth, and Nicolas Fontaine took sixth place. The silver and bronze medal for Laroche and Langlois was only the second time ever that two Canadians had stood on the podium in an individual Winter Olympic event.

Mogul Master Jean-Luc Brassard

Looking up at any mogul run, all the average weekend skier sees is an automatic knee injury. The mogul runs are for the expert or for the sheer insane. But a few athletes out there don't see the moguls but instead see the paths around them, and Québec's Jean-Luc Brassard was one of Canada's best. His sport does require a little bit of insanity but also huge amounts of style, grace and speed, all qualities that Brassard possessed.

Growing up in a two-storey house on the banks of the St. Lawrence River, Brassard first discovered the sport of freestyle skiing when he saw the televised acrobatics of pioneer freestyle ski jumpers Yves and Dom Laroche, part of the Québec Air Force. Watching the Québec duo perform hair-raising feats off snow-covered mounds and soar through the air at incredible speeds, the wide-eyed youngster knew he had to be a part of this sport somehow. But there was just one problem. No real mountains were near his home. But that did not stop the resourceful young Brassard.

Family photos clearly show to what lengths he would go to realize his dreams. One winter he took his father's ladder from the garage and leaned it up against the house. Then he laid boards over the spaces and watered the whole thing down to get a flat surface. After packing snow over the track, Brassard had constructed his own freestyle platform to practice on at home. While neighbours were playing hockey on backyard rinks, he was trying to fly into the air.

"What I had was something like a backyard rink on a steep angle," recalled Brassard.

As a teenager he moved from the backyard to the slopes and began to quickly show how much all that practice had paid off. The aerial stunts of the Québec Air Force were a little too extreme for Brassard, but the moguls were the perfect event for his combination of skills and daring.

By 1992 he was at the top of the sport, winning the gold medal at the World Championships. Brassard also tried out his skills at the 1992 Winter Games in Albertville, France. Although he had the talent required to win the gold medal, he was still young, and the pressure of competition at the Olympic level took him off his game. He finished in seventh place.

"When I took my position in the starting gate, all I could see were the red lights on the cameras pointing at me," Brassard recalled. "I could hear people clapping, and I was thinking, whew, it's time to put on a show. But I think I tried too hard that morning. I think I got too intense. And at the bottom, after it was over, I knew I could have done much better."

The 1992 Winter Games was a wake-up call for the brash young skier. During the wait for the 1994 Games in Lillehammer, Brassard set himself to work on perfecting his craft. Over the next two years, he worked his way to the top of the world mogul circuit and was able to knock off reigning champion Eddy Grospiron of France. The Frenchman was the one who took home gold in Albertville, and he ruled the slopes in the World Championships, but now it was time for a changing of the guard.

It was also in between 1992 and 1994 that Brassard fell in love with another Olympian. When he met figure skater Isabelle Brasseur, they immediately connected and began dating, but the relationship faced many different obstacles from the start. Isabelle was going through a tough time professionally and with her family life. In January 1992 her grandfather passed away. At the 1992 Games in Albertville she fell while performing with her skating partner Lloyd Eisler, most likely costing the pair the gold or silver medal. After the Olympics her performance was again substandard at the World Championships, and the pair came up short of the gold. It was also in March of that year that her father died. It was a difficult year for Isabelle and Jean-Luc, but the couple saw each other through, and she was waiting at the bottom of the hill as Brassard prepared to take a shot at gold at the 1994 Games in Lillehammer.

The moguls event always attracts a lot of media attention because of the daredevil nature of the sport, and the world's eyes were focused on Brassard's run for the gold. He had easily made it through the preliminary rounds and was up against his French rival in the final medal round. Eddy Grospiron went first. But after his run, the judges had him in second place. The leader was a relative unknown on the mogul circuit, a Russian named Sergei Shupletsov who had racked up a point total of 26.90. Brassard had scored better marks in earlier competitions, but this was the Olympics, and he didn't want to fool himself into that same false sense of security that had him finish in seventh in 1992.

History would not repeat itself. Brassard bounced off the moguls like his knees were made of shock absorbers. On the second jump of the run, he performed a flawless version of a move called the Iron Cross-Cossack combination that had become known as his specialty. He completed the run in 24.5 seconds. Even before the judges had put up his scores, Brassard knew that he had had the run of his career. When the score showed 27.24 points, he pumped his fists in the air and hugged Isabelle, who had watched the run from the sidelines. He had just won the gold medal, Canada's first of those Games and the first for him.

Freestyle Skier Chris Del Bosco

The story of Chris Del Bosco's journey to the 2010 Olympics could be a movie made for Hollywood. The Canadian Olympic ski-cross athlete did not always have such a promising future.

Born to move, as soon as young Chris learned how to walk he was learning how to ski. Born and raised in the picturesque hills of Vail, Colorado, 27-year-old Chris had plenty of activities to keep him busy growing up. In the winter he spent his time blazing down pro-runs and sailing into the air off moguls, and in the summer he traded his skis for a bike and tore up the hillside. Thanks to his father's Canadian citizenship, Chris was allowed to join the Canadian team and has fully embraced his Canadian heritage.

But his need for the adrenaline rush followed him off the mountainside. "I was kind of a party kid," Del Bosco said in a recent interview with the *Star*. "I just loved to live life in the fast lane with everything. Go fast skiing and then go hang out partying....It was getting bad. I was drinking a lot. Everybody had kind of given up on me."

When he began drinking, his talents on the mountain fell by the wayside, and the young athlete was in danger of ruining his career. Drinking had complete control of his life. Although some people are able to have a few drinks and quit, Del Bosco just could not stop.

Things got so bad that a stranger once found him passed out in a ditch with a broken neck. Finally, with a little help from friends, Chris started getting his life back on track, but he also needed help restarting his career. It took help from some Canadians.

It just so happened that the Canadian ski-cross team was looking for a skier to fill their lineup. The wife of Del Bosco's cousin knew the CEO of the Canadian ski team; it was the perfect fit. Since then, he has been racing for the Canadian ski team and has been sober for two years.

With his life back on track and the 2010 Olympics fast approaching, Del Bosco looks to the future with a positive attitude. "I just kind of took a little different path and now I'm kind of refocused onto that dream again," said Del Bosco. "My life couldn't be better right now. Either way, Olympics or not, I just couldn't be luckier."

Freestyle Skier Jenn Heil

Canada's female veteran of the freestyle slopes, Jenn Heil is no longer just happy to be at the Olympics and go for a personal best. She is dropping the "nice gal" Canadian façade and going for gold. For the 26-year-old native of Spruce Grove, Alberta, competing in front of her fellow Canadian citizens is an opportunity not to be missed.

"I see this as an opportunity for Canada," Heil said in an interview with Canadian Press. "I really feel like we're making the shift and the attitude change toward excellence in our country. Yes, it's focused on sport, but it's so much bigger than that. Focusing on excellence, building the programs that support it, that's cultural. That can be in the sciences. That can be in the arts. That can be everywhere. I think it's really important that Canadians are embracing that. I've seen a big shift since when I made the national team in 2001. We're saying, 'We want to go out there, we want to perform, we want to win.' I find that an amazing thing. I see it as the future of the country."

This kind of confidence, however, did not always come so easily. When Heil first branched out into the world of international competitive freestyle skiing, no one knew her name, and she wasn't very good. She made her first foray to the World Cup on December 5, 1999, and ended up finishing 29th out of 30 competitors in the moguls event. But the young freestyle skier was not about to give up after one race. Just two years later, she was skiing to podium finishes in races all over the world and by 2002 had earned a spot on the Canadian Olympic freestyle ski team. At that time just 18 years old, the mogul skier was one of Canada's top young hopefuls at the games. Heil put in an inspiring series of runs but came up short with a fourth-place finish overall. She missed a bronze medal by just 0.01 seconds.

More success followed on the World Cup circuit, but it was Olympic gold that she wanted. Going into the 2006 Games in Turin, Heil was Canada's best hope for a medal, but the international field offered some stiff competition. Most notable among them was reigning Olympic champion Kari Traa of Norway. Undaunted by the task ahead, Heil bounced off the moguls as if her knees were made of springs and finished her run well ahead of the Olympic champion. It was only day two of the Turin Games, and Heil had just won Canada's first gold of the Olympics and the first Olympic mogul medal won by a Canadian woman. But there seemed to have been some confusion with the Italian announcers, because when Heil accepted her medal, they announced her as being American. Heil laughed at the error; after all, it didn't really matter, because she was an Olympic champion.

As Vancouver 2010 creeps closer and closer, Heil remains focused and determined to show the world that Canadians can not only be gracious hosts but they can own the podium as well. "For me, I am really focused on what I need to do to get strong physically,'" Heil said.

Cross-country Skier Chandra Crawford

When a young Chandra Crawford watched as Myriam Bedard accepted her two gold medals at the Olympics in 1994, she immediately took up the sport of biathlon, hoping to one day be like her heroine. Crawford competed for five years as a biathlete, but her marksmanship was not at the level where she could compete with the best in the world, and at the age of 16 she made the switch to cross-country skiing and has never looked back.

Now focused on only one area, Crawford began to move up the competitive ladder. After making her mark on the national cross-country ski scene—placing first in sprint at the Canadian Championships in 2003 and again in 2005—her Canadian results qualified her for World Cup competition, and in 2006 she placed third in the sprint category. Riding high on her World Cup performance, she went into the 2006 Turin Games as Canada's best hope to win a cross-country medal. The sweet blonde from Canmore, Alberta, did not disappoint.

Going into the sprint event, Crawford was not on anyone's radar to take home a medal, let alone to win the gold. Canadians had pinned greater hopes on her teammates Beckie Scott and Sara Renner. But when Crawford crossed the finish line in first place, no one would doubt her again.

Entering the 2010 Games as the reigning Olympic gold medallist, Crawford has already proven that she can win and now looks to establish herself as one of the best in the sport in Olympic history. But she has faced some challenges. In February 2009, the 25-year-old had to undergo surgery to her lower leg because of a nagging condition that restricted the blood supply to her shins. Yet despite having to remain off her skis for several months, Crawford remained philosophical about her situation: "If I have learned anything as an athlete, it's that the great highs are born out of the motivation I get after a deep low, and I will be the most excited, grateful, motivated and rested girl out there on skis once I get through this," she said.

It is with this positive attitude and strong will that she will attempt to repeat as Olympic sprint gold medallist and maybe more when 2010 Vancouver rolls around.

Ski Jumping: Trevor Morrice and Stefan Read

In the history of the Winter Games, no Canadian has ever won a ski-jumping medal. But that hasn't stopped 2010 hopefuls Trevor Morrice and Stefan Read, both of Calgary, Alberta. Just getting the chance to compete among the best athletes in the world is something that both athletes have been looking forward to since they first strapped on skis and launched themselves into the air. It's a privilege that neither of them takes for granted, because ski jumping was nearly removed as an Olympic event.

When the Olympic lineup of events was initially announced, women ski jumpers around the world learned the bad news that they would not be participating at the 2010 Games and that the men would. It was a decision that the women did not take lightly. A group of current and former women jumpers got together and sued the Vancouver Olympic organizers in April 2009, arguing that keeping the women's events out is a direct violation of the Canadian Charter of Rights and Freedoms. They were calling for the British Columbian Supreme Court to declare that if they were not included, the men's event should be excluded too.

Although Read supported the aims of his women peers, his desire to participate in the Games outweighed that support. "Ski jumping in Europe is way too big for that to actually pass," said Read. "There will be a lot of angry people and a lot more lawyers after that one lawyer if that was the case."

Luckily for Read and Morrice, the Olympic Committee won the decision in court. The rules to gain entry into the Olympics are that a sport must hold a World Championship prior to the decision on the Olympic program. Since the women had not participated in a World Championship, they were left off the Vancouver program.

With the legal issues out of the way, both Read and Morrice are looking forward to gaining some experience at their first Olympics. While it is unlikely that either of them will make it to the podium, both are under 25 and will have long and fruitful careers ahead of them.

Nordic Combined

Not many people are aware of the Nordic combined event at the Olympic Games, but it has been around since the 1924 Winter Games and is a highly sought-after medal by the Scandinavian countries. Norway has led the medal count since 1924, with 26 in total, and Finland comes in second with 14 overall. Nordic combined is part of the ski events and is basically the joining of cross-country skiing and ski jumping into one sport. Canada has never won a medal in this event, but that doesn't mean our athletes have stopped trying. On the top of that list is Canada's Jason Myslicki.

At the 2006 Olympic Games, Myslicki and Canadian teammate Max Thompson became Canada's first athletes in the Nordic event since the 1988 Games in Calgary. It wasn't that Canada did not have athletes to send, it was just that they were not meeting the international standard of competition. For 2006, the Canadian Olympic Committee decided to relax certain rules and allow the young Canadian athletes a chance to gain some experience. Myslicki finished 41st in both individual events but was simply glad to participate. "This sport sucks. It sucks, but I love it," said Myslicki in an interview after the Games. "It has been such a long road to get here, so this meant something. Nobody knows what we do. Nobody knows who we are. We don't get a lot of support or anything. We just love it."

Well, not much has changed for the 2010 Olympics; people in Canada don't know his name and few know anything about the sport. But Myslicki and teammate Wesley Savill will be Canada's lone hopes on the hill. Canadians might not know the sport, but when Myslicki and Savill's names are announced in Vancouver, they will certainly feel welcomed.

2010 Olympic Snow Sports

2010 Olympic Alpine Skiing Schedule

Location: Whistler, BC
Medal Ceremonies: Whistler Village Celebration Plaza

Whistler Mountain (capacity: 7600)

February 13: Men's downhill
February 14: Women's super combined
February 16: Men's super combined
February 17: Women's downhill
February 19: Men's super-G
February 20: Women's super-G
February 21: Men's giant slalom
February 24: Women's giant slalom
February 26: Women's slalom
February 27: Men's slalom

2010 Olympic Cross-country Skiing Schedule

Location: Callaghan Valley, west of Whistler, BC

Medal Ceremonies: Whistler Village Celebration Plaza

Whistler Olympic Park, Callaghan Valley, (capacity: 12,000)

February 15: Men's 15-kilometre individual; women's 10-kilometre individual

February 17: Men's and women's 1500-metre sprint

February 19: Women's 7.5-kilometre × 2 pursuit

February 20: Men's 15-kilometre × 2 pursuit

February 22: Men's and women's team pursuit

February 24: Men's 4 × 10-kilometre relay

February 25: Women's 4 × 5-kilometre relay

February 27: Women's 30-kilometre mass start

February 28: Men's 50-kilometre mass start

2010 Olympic Biathlon Schedule

Location: Callaghan Valley, west of Whistler, BC

Medal Ceremonies: Whistler Village Celebration Plaza

Whistler Olympic Park, Callaghan Valley, (capacity: 12,000)

February 13: Women's 7.5-kilometre sprint

February 14: Men's 10-kilometre sprint

February 16: Men's 12.5-kilometre pursuit; Women's 10-kilometre pursuit

February 18: Men's 20-kilometre individual; Women's
15-kilometre individual
February 21: Men's 15-kilometre mass start; Women's
12.5-kilometre mass start
February 23: Women's 4 × 6-kilometre relay
February 26: Men's 4 × 7.5-kilometre relay

2010 Olympic Freestyle Skiing Schedule

Location: West Vancouver, BC
Medal Ceremonies: BC Place Stadium

Cypress Mountain (capacity 8000)

February 13: Women's moguls
February 14: Men's moguls
February 20: Women's aerials, qualifying
February 21: Men's ski cross
February 22: Men's aerials, qualifying
February 23: Women's ski cross
February 24: Women's aerials, finals
February 25: Men's aerials, finals

2010 Ski Jumping and Nordic Combined Schedule

Location: Callaghan Valley, west of Whistler, BC
Medal Ceremonies: Whistler Village Celebration
Plaza
Whistler Olympic Park, Callaghan Valley, (capacity:
12,000)

February 12: Men's Normal-hill qualifying, individual

February 13: Men's Normal-hill final, individual

February 14: Men's Nordic combined normal hill, individual

February 19: Men's Large-hill final, individual

February 20: Men's Large-hill final, individual

February 22: Men's Large hill, team

February 23: Nordic combined team large hill

February 25: Men's Nordic combined large hill, sprint

2010 Olympic Snowboarding Schedule

Location: West Vancouver, BC
Medal Ceremonies: BC Place Stadium

Cypress Mountain (capacity 8000)

February 15: Men's snowboard cross

February 16: Women's snowboard cross

February 17: Men's snowboard halfpipe

February 18: Women's snowboard halfpipe

February 26: Women's snowboard parallel giant slalom

February 27: Men's snowboard parallel giant slalom

Chapter Seven

On the Ice: Curling, Bobsleigh, Skeleton and Luge

When curling was introduced into the Olympic program, many said that it didn't belong because it was not really a sport. Those were all people who have likely never played the game. Sport is not just about who can run faster or jump higher; it takes skill, intelligence and experience, all elements that are necessary to succeed in curling. Since 1998, when curling was introduced as an Olympic event, Canadian curlers have always challenged for the top spot on the podium, and come 2010, Canada will send its best and brightest to win gold before the home crowds.

Canadians will also get to view some of the most dramatic moments in other Winter Olympic events, which occur on the ice tracks in the sports of bobsleigh, luge and skeleton. It's not hard to understand why when you first see athletes willingly launch themselves down a winding icy track on the side of a mountain. Although the athletes in these events use the same track, the three sports are considerably different.

Bobsleigh is the most recognizable of the three sports because it has been part of the Games program from the first Olympics, although the sleds used in 1924 looked quite different from the ones that will hit the tracks at the 2010 Vancouver Games. Whereas the sleighs of today look like carbon fibre missiles, in 1924 it was simply four men sitting on a padded seat attached to sets of blades.

Although the equipment has changed greatly, the mechanics of the sport remain the same: teams of two or four men sit on a sleigh and steer through an icy downhill course.

Canada has never faired very well in the bobsleigh event, winning only three medals in Olympic history. The first was a gold won by Vic Emery, John Emery, Douglas Anakin and Peter Kirby at the 1964 Games in Innsbruck, Austria; another gold was won at the 1998 Games by Pierre Lueders and Dave MacEachern in the two-man event; and a silver at the 2006 Games was won again by Pierre Lueders and his new partner, Lascelles Brown.

In the sport of luge, athletes lie down on their backs on a sled and propel themselves down the track feet first, steering the sled with the movement of their bodies and the force of gravity. Although the sport has been around since the early 1800s, it wasn't added to the Olympic calendar until the 1964 Games in Innsbruck.

Canada has never won a medal in the luge event. The sport is dominated by the Germans, the Austrians and the Swiss, but a new group of Canadian athletes hopes to break that supremacy before a home crowd in 2010.

The skeleton event is similar to luge, but with one major difference: athletes lie on their stomachs and hurtle down the icy course face first. It's fast and dangerous, and the crowds love it.

Schmirler the Curler

Canada has never had a more popular curling figure than Sandra Schmirler—a figure who became a household name after winning Canada's first gold medal in curling in 1998 and one that a nation mourned when she passed away in 2000 after a battle with cancer.

On the ice, she captured the attention of Canadian curling fans when her team won the Canadian Scott Tournament of Hearts in 1993 and then later went on to win on the international stage with a gold medal at the World Championships in 1993 as well. But the path to the top did not happen overnight. It started many years earlier, in Biggar, Saskatchewan, when she and her two sisters were introduced to the game by their parents.

Already a gifted athlete as a child, playing volleyball, badminton and softball, Schmirler continued to pursue her love for those sports, but curling gradually became her true passion. She got to be so good at the sport that she entered into the provincial championships and won in her very first appearance in 1987. She eventually moved up the curling ladder and by 1993 was a national and world champion.

Schmirler had quickly carved out a reputation for herself as one of the planet's greatest curlers of all-time. In a nutshell, she was a brilliant tactician, a dominant shooter and a commanding leader. As the ever-candid

Canadian curler Colleen Jones once said about playing against Schmirler, "When you played her, you were in awe. You knew she was better. You knew she was going to beat you. It was like playing against Gretzky."

A three-time Canadian and World Champion, Schmirler also won the first women's Olympic gold in 1998. More than anything else, this triumph thrust her not only into the national spotlight but also the international spotlight. The inclusion of curling as a full medal Olympic sport in 1998 has propelled the game onto the global stage, and in many ways Schmirler became curling's first global ambassador. After some of her games in Nagano, she would linger over a few beers and explain the intricacies of the game to confused foreign reporters and puzzled Japanese fans for whom curling appeared to be nothing more than a chaos of smashing rocks.

It was after the birth of her second daughter in 1999 that Schmirler's life took an unexpected turn for the worse when she was diagnosed with cancer. Given her stature in Canada, people wanted to know how she was doing, and when she spoke about her grave condition, Schmirler provided her fans with a heartwarming perspective. In 2000, while working as a commentator for the CBC during a junior curling game in Moncton, she held a press conference to address her condition.

"There were three goals I had coming out of this thing, and the first one was to look after my family.

And the second one...because I curl so much, I've never taken a hot vacation, so I'm going to put my feet in the sand in a warm place. And the last one was to actually be here today."

Not long after the press conference, Sandra Schmirler died at the age of 36. Her impact on curling and Canada was such that Prime Minister Jean Chretien spoke of her "bright, engaging, personality" and her incredible zest for life. She was so popular that her funeral was even broadcast on national television. Sadly and ironically, her struggle with cancer and subsequent death played a role in bringing curling into the spotlight.

In that final press conference, her competitive spirit was put aside for just a moment when she stated, "I now know losing a curling game isn't the end of the world."

Jennifer Jones

Now the undisputed queen of Canadian curling, Jennifer Jones has won all significant curling tournaments, except one: Olympic gold. The 35-year-old native of Winnipeg, Manitoba, burst onto the curling scene in 1994 when she won the Canadian Junior Curling Championships, and she has been on a steady rise ever since.

In 2002, she got her first big break into the world of high-stakes curling when she won the Manitoba Women's Curling Championship and earned the right to go to the 2002 Scott Tournament of Hearts. The tournament is the premiere Canadian curling event. A win there and you earn the honour of representing Canada at the World Championships. Although she played well in the round robin, winning eight matches with only three losses, Ontario skip Sherry Middaugh knocked Jones out of contention in the first match of the playoffs.

It wasn't until 2005 that Jones returned to the Scott Tournament. Jones, along with Cathy Overton, Jill Officer and Cathy Gauthier, dominated the tournament, losing only twice in the round robin and defeating skip Jenn Hanna in a game that came down to the last rock. Hanna and her team had control of the game from the outset and looked like they could walk away with the title. However, in the final end of the game, Jones pulled off an incredible shot that gave her four points and the victory. It was a great honour for Jones, and she wanted to take that success with her into the World Championship as the

Canadian women's representative. But it was a disappointing tournament overall. She wasn't making the shots when she needed, and the choppy ice gave her problems in all her games. She finished the round robin with a record of 8-3, but in the first round of the playoffs she allowed Norwegian skip Dordi Nordby to score 10 unanswered points and steal the game 12-5, thus eliminating her from the medal rounds.

Jones could not repeat as champion in 2006 at the Scotts Tournament, but 2008 was a much better year. After winning the provincial tournament, she beat Alberta's Shannon Kleibrink to win the Scotts, and then at the World Curling Championship, she beat the Chinese in the final to take home her first title. It was Team Canada's second championship in a row, and Jones received a call from Prime Minister Stephen Harper to congratulate her, saying,

Along with all Canadians, I am extremely proud of the outstanding performance by our women's curling team. Their exciting play throughout the tournament coupled with some close final end victories proved that Canadian players have the talent and grit to overcome adversity and emerge as champions.

In 2009, she repeated as the Scotts champion and as the reigning queen of Canadian curling. Her intelligent play and series of victories have earned her a spot on the team that will be representing Canada at the 2010 Olympics. She is hoping to return Olympic gold to Canada since the time Sandra Schmirler won at the 1998 Nagano Games.

Olympic Rivalry: Glenn Howard vs. Kevin Martin

Ever since curling was added to the Olympic calendar in 1998, Canada has always been one of the countries to continually produce world-class athletes—such as first-ever women's Olympic champion Sandra Schmirler and 2006 Olympic gold medallist Brad Gushue. For the 2010 Olympics, the Canadian men's team looks like they could once again contend with the likes of Glenn Howard and Kevin Martin vying for the rights to represent Canada in Vancouver.

Both Martin and Howard are longtime veterans of Canadian and international curling and hold numerous titles among them, including World Curling Champion (Martin in 2008, Howard in 1987, 1993 and 2007) and one Olympic silver medal won by Martin at the 2002 Salt Lake City Games.

Kevin Martin has made a name for himself as one of the most successful international curlers in the world. He first appeared on the scene in 1985 when he won the Canadian Junior Championship, and he has not looked back ever since. Before his official experience at the 2002 Olympic Games, where he won a silver medal, he had made an appearance at the 1992 Albertville Olympics, when curling was just a demonstration sport. A younger Martin was only able to come in fourth place. Ten years later he was back at the Olympics, but this time with a lot more experience and talent. At the

2002 Olympics he completely dominated his opponents in the preliminary rounds, winning nine of 10 games. But the incredible record was all for naught when he lost the gold medal in the finals to Norwegian skip Pal Trulsen. In the last round, all Martin had to do was make one final draw to win the gold medal, but his rock went off course, and Norway walked away with the gold. Ever since that moment, Martin has wanted to return to the Olympics and prove that he can finally make that gold-medal-winning shot.

Glenn Howard, however, has never been to the big Olympic show and would like nothing more than to add that to his resumé. He has had success at all levels of curling, but it was his brother, Russ, who was able to bring home the gold in 2006 along with skip Brad Gushue. Through much of his early career Glenn played with Russ, and the siblings won several Brier tournaments as well as the World Championships in 1987 and 1993. But in the late 1990s the brothers went their separate ways, and Glenn Howard got a team of his own out of Ontario. Since then he has skipped his way to Brier championships and World Championships, but it's the Olympics that remain uncharted territory for the 47-year-old Ontario native. He just has to take all other competitors out of his way.

Most recently, the two curling greats of Martin and Howard have battled it out for Canadian supremacy in the finals of the 2008 Tim Horton's Brier. The two titans of the ice played a close game, but it was Martin who came out the victor by a final score of 5–4. Howard, however, would not be denied his revenge when they again met up at the Tylenol Players' Championship, where Howard earned a berth at the 2009 Olympic trials by shellacking Martin with a 7–1 win.

A long list of other curling teams will be at the 2009 Canadian Olympic trials, but if Howard and Martin get the chance to meet in the finals, then Canadian curling fans can rest assured that they will be sending one of the greatest curlers this nation has.

2010 Olympic Curling Schedule

Location: Vancouver, BC
Medal Ceremonies: BC Place Stadium

Vancouver Olympic/Paralympic Centre, adjacent to Queen Elizabeth Park (capacity: 6000)

February 16–23: Men and Women's curling, three draws daily
February 24: Men and Women's tiebreakers
February 25: Men and Women's semifinals
February 26: Women's medal round
February 27: Men's medal round

Bobsleigh Champs

When Vic Emery first saw the bobsleigh event at the 1956 Olympics, he immediately fell in love with the sport. Although a majority of Canadians had never heard of the sport, and Canada did not even have a track for athletes to practice on, Emery knew he had to get a team together for the 1964 Games in Innsbruck, Austria. He found willing partners in his brother John, and friends Peter Kirby and Doug Anakin. Although new to the sport of bobsled, each man was already an accomplished athlete.

During his university days, Vic Emery was a member of the swimming, wrestling and skiing teams and also had some Olympic experience as a Finn sailor. His brother John was an all-round athlete who won the Duke of Edinburgh Trophy for the best all-round athlete in the Royal Canadian Navy Reserve. Peter Kirby had been captain of his Darmouth college ski team and was a member of the 1954 Canadian ski team at the World Championships. Doug Anakin was a professional-level skier, an avid mountain climber and, in his college days, a wrestling champion.

The four men had the necessary will and the athletic training, but they just happened to come from a country with no bobsled training facilities, no organization and, most importantly, no tracks. So prior to the Olympics, the men practiced largely on dry land and in gymnasiums, working on their starts, their form going down the runs and their general physical development. In comparison, the Austrian, Italian and Swiss teams had access to the actual course they would compete on in the Olympics for weeks in advance.

In terms of the actual time they spent bobsleighing, the Canadian men were able to take a few runs down North America's only bobsleigh run, in Lake Placid, New York, as well as four practice runs in Innsbruck before the actual start of the Games. At the time, it was conventional to put heavier athletes in the bobsleds, with the understanding that the extra weight translated into momentum down the course. But Vic Emery thought differently. He knew the key to winning was an excellent start and control through the turns.

In their first run in Olympic competition, the four Canadian men broke the Olympic track record. But it was almost a disaster. Near the end of the run, one of their axles seized, and they almost overturned. Only by moving their bodies in unison did they prevent an accident and keep their hopes alive of winning gold. In a sport where hundredths of a second separate first from fourth, the Canadian crew nearly had a full second lead on the Austrian team after the first run.

Vic Emery recalled the event in the book *Canada: Our Century in Sport*:

After the first four-man heat in which we broke the record which was never broken afterwards, my teammates discovered that a rear axle had seized as we caromed off the second last corner into the finishing straight. While I walked the run, my Italian mentor, Eugenio Monti, lying in third place at the time, called his mechanics over and by the time I reached the top for our second run, they had partially fixed it—good enough to get us down with the second fastest second heat and a substantial lead overall.

The Canadians came in second again in the next heat, and three days later they piloted the fastest run to win the gold medal by a margin of one second. It was one of the greatest upsets of the 1964 Winter Olympics.

Vic Emery remembered the chemistry of his teammates and why they won the gold that day.

We were all rounded sportsmen who wanted to see how far we could go in a sport that didn't interfere with our careers. With only natural tracks, bobsledding had a short season then and gave us challenge, excitement and international camaraderie. It also seemed to suit me as a driver from my background in aerobatic flying in the Navy and so used to snow and ice in Canada's winter from car driving to ice hockey.

To prove their success was not just a one-time fluke, the four-man team captured the 1965 World Championship title in St. Moritz and defeated the favoured Italians by a full two seconds.

Pierre Lueders

There is no doubt that Pierre Lueders is Canada's greatest bobsled athlete of all time. Unlike a lot of other Canadian athletes going into the 2010 Games, Lueder's resumé of victories goes far back.

Starting in 1997 Lueders and brakeman Dave MacEachern established their presence as one of the best two-man teams in the world by winning the over-all World Cup title. It was an incredible achievement for the Canadian bobsled program that had not seen very good results since Vic Emery and his four-man bobsled won gold at the 1964 Games. But the World Cup finish was just the beginning for Lueders.

At the 1998 Olympics in Nagano, Lueders announced the return of Canadian bobsledding. Now placed among the top in the world, he was one of the favou-rites to walk away from the Olympics with a medal.

But Italian sledder Guenther Huber had his eyes on the gold medal as well. After the first two runs, Lueders found himself just 0.04 seconds behind the Italian. In the third run, he reduced that margin slightly to 0.03 seconds.

Prior to the start of the fourth and final run of the event, Lueders approached Huber in the start house and joked about the possible results: "Can you imagine if we tied this thing? It would be incredible." The pre-diction came true—Lueders and MacEachern shared their gold medal with the Italian team. It was a major accomplishment for Lueders, but he wasn't done yet.

Lueders continued to have success on the World Cup tour, winning several gold and silver medals from 1998 to 2004. The 2002 Olympics in Salt Lake City were a disappointment as he finished off the podium in both the two- and four-man sled competitions. In need of a new direction, Lueders began training with brakeman Lascelles Brown in 2004, and the pair saw immediate success on the World Cup tour, winning the two-man title in 2005. At the Olympics in 2006, Lueders and Brown placed a disappointing fifth place after the first run but managed to come back and win a silver medal.

For the 2010 Games, the 39-year-old athlete knows this will be his last shot at an Olympic medal, but that when it comes to racing, he is all business.

"One thing I really wanted to do this year was look back at the things I did when I had seasons where I felt the best prepared," said Lueders. "I've picked what I think are the best elements of my past training and put them together."

Paired alongside Edmonton Eskimos running back Jesse Lumsden as his brakeman in the two-man and four-man events, Lueders could end his Olympic career before a home crowd.

Skeleton

Although luge is the more recognized of the winter track sports, the skeleton event was actually a part of the 1928 Games in St. Moritz, Switzerland. The event made another appearance at the 1948 Games in St. Moritz before disappearing again until the 2002 Games in Salt Lake City, where it now appears to have secured a permanent place on the Olympic calendar. The course starts with the athletes taking a running start by pushing their sled down a few metres of track before diving onto the sled. Athletes must lie prone, facing downhill, with their arms at their sides and using only their bodies and the force of gravity to steer the sled.

Canada has never faired well in bobsleigh or luge competition, but ever since the sport of skeleton was introduced back into the Olympics in 2002, Canadian athletes have been carving out a place in the international spotlight. Although Canada did not win a medal at the Salt Lake City Games, our athletes were able to gain a level of international experience they would need when they returned to the Olympic stage in 2006. Such athletes included two-time World Cup medallist Paul Boehm, World Champion Jeff Pain, Canadian Champion Jon Montgomery, and Canadian and World Cup medallist Mellisa Hollingsworth.

The team had consistently finished on the world stage in the top 10 and was always just a few hundredths of a second off a gold-medal win. It was only a matter of time before success would arrive at the Olympics, but no one had predicted it would come so soon and that so many would stand on the podium.

Up first on the podium in the 2006 Olympics in Turin, Italy, was Duff Gibson. At 39 years of age, he was not given much chance of beating a much younger field of athletes, but experience won out over youth, and he took home the gold medal in the men's event. Gibson just happened to beat young Canadian Jeff Pain, who put in an equally amazing performance to take home the silver. On the women's side, Mellisa Hollingsworth slid to a bronze-medal finish. Three medals in one sport in one Olympics was an incredible result for the Canadian team in Turin, but in 2010, Canada will be looking for more.

Mellisa Hollingsworth, a 29-year-old native of Eckville, Alberta, almost quit the sport in 2002 when she wasn't named to the Canadian Olympic team, but thankfully for her and the rest of Canada, she decided to stay in the sport that she loved. After becoming the first Canadian medallist in skeleton in 2006 in Turin, she has continued to make her mark on the World Cup circuit with several finishes in the top three and the 2007–08 Canadian Championship. When not pursuing her dreams of Olympic gold and athletic perfection, Hollingsworth can be found on a ranch riding horses or down at a local rodeo. In fact, horse riding was her first love; she was only introduced to skeleton later in life by her cousin, Ryan Davenport, a two-time World Skeleton champion. Luckily for Canadians, she not only immediately took to the sport but she also began winning races. Her success came from her training and in part from her attitude when approaching each match.

"I no longer hit the start line to participate in races. I'm now focused on sliding to the podium and winning each time I put on the Canadian uniform," said Hollingsworth. She takes that attitude with her to the top of the mountains in Vancouver in hopes of winning gold for her country.

2010 Olympic Bobsled, Luge and Skeleton Schedule

Location: Whistler, BC
Medal Ceremonies: Whistler Village Plaza

Whistler Sliding Centre, Blackcomb Mountain
(capacity: 12,000)

February 13–14: Men's luge
February 15–16: Women's luge
February 17: Doubles luge
February 18–19: Men's and Women's skeleton
February 20–21: Two-man bobsled
February 23–24: Women's bobsled
February 26–27: Four-man bobsled

Chapter Eight

Quick Facts and Stats

Quick Facts

- Canada won its first gold medal in hockey during the 1920 Summer Games (see chapter three for further details).

- In the history of hockey at the Winter Olympic Games, Canada has won nine gold medals (including the 1920 Summer Games gold medal), five silver medals and two bronze medals. The Soviet Union/Russia comes in second place with eight gold medals, two silver medals and two bronze medals.

- Canada sent the most competitors in its Winter Olympic history to the 2006 Games in Turin, Italy: 195 athletes competing in 15 sports.

- The 2006 Turin Games were also where Canada had its best showing, winning seven gold, 10 silver and seven bronze medals, for a total of 24 medals. The medal count was pushed to its highest level thanks to speed skater Cindy Klassen's five medals. Not only did Canada increase its total medal count from the previous Winter Games of 2002 for the seventh straight time (since 1980), but the total medal count was also the "best ever" for Canada for the fifth straight time (since 1992). Canada won at least one medal in 10 of the 15 sport disciplines competed in at the Games, and gold medals in six different disciplines; both feats were unmatched by any other nation. Canada also had the most fourth- and fifth-place finishes (14 and nine respectively) of any country in these games.

• Cindy Klassen holds four Canadian speed skating records, in the 1000-metre, 1500-metre, 3000-metre and 5000-metre events. Her times in the 1000 metre, 1500 metre and the 3000 metre are also world records. Klassen is also the Canadian record holder in most medals won at the Olympics (Summer and Winter), with six medals in total: one medal in 2002 and five at the 2006 Winter Games.

• Canada's greatest speed skater Marc Gagnon has won 35 World Championship medals but will always be most well known for winning five medals at the Olympic Games. He earned one bronze medal at the 1994 Games in Lillehammer, one gold at the 1998 Nagano Games, and two gold and one bronze at the 2002 Salt Lake City Games, for a total of five, tying Canadian runner Phil Edwards for the most medals won by a Canadian male at the Olympic Games.

• At the age of 50, Russ Howard became Canada's oldest gold medallist when he and fellow teammates Brad Gushue, Jamie Korab, Mark Nichols and Mike Adam took the curling title at the 2006 Games in Italy.

• When Vancouver hosts the 2010 Winter Games, it will be only the second time Canada has hosted the Games. The only other time was 1988, when Calgary held the Games. Québec City attempted to win the Games in 2002, but lost out to Salt Lake City.

• Alex Hurd became the first Canadian to win a medal at the 1932 Winter Games, other than hockey, when he won the bronze medal in the 500-metre speed skating event.

• Canadian figure skater Kurt Browning was the first to successfully complete a quadruple toe loop at the figure skating world championships in Budapest, Hungary, in 1988.

• The first figure skaters from Canada to win a medal in ice dancing at the Olympic Winter Games was pairs skaters Tracy Wilson and Robert McCall, who won a bronze medal before a hometown crowd on February 23 at the 1988 Games in Calgary, Alberta.

• The first speed skater to skate the 1000 metres in under 1:10 minutes was Sylvain Bouchard, who sped to a time of 1:09.60 seconds in Calgary, Alberta, on March 29, 1998.

• At the 1948 Olympics in St. Mortiz, Switzerland, the Canadian Olympic hockey team (RCAF Flyers) were playing a game against the Swedes. In the third period, the Canadian goaltender Murray Dowey caught the puck and passed it forward to his defenseman. At the time, this was against the rules of international hockey (the puck had to be put behind the net after a save). Dowey was given a two-minute penalty and had to serve the time in the bow. Defenseman Andre Laperriere took Dowey's gloves and stick and played goal for the remainder of the game. This was the only time in Olympic history that such a peculiarity has occurred.

• At the 1952 Olympics, Team Canada goaltender Ralph Hansch became the only player ever to wear the number "0" in an Olympic hockey tournament. After the Olympics (which saw Canada bring home the gold), the IOC added a new rule that said future wearing of the digit was illegal.

• During the hockey tournament at the 1956 Olympics in Cortina d'Ampezzo, Italy, European referees were having trouble keeping up with the pace of the game and therefore were missing many penalties. The problem got so bad that International Ice Hockey Federation European president Bunny Ahearne proposed an insane way to rectify the problem.

His solution involved putting the refs in a cage of sorts suspended above the ice so as to have a better vantage point of the entire ice surface. He elaborated further in a memo to the IIHF board, "A spotlight would follow the referee up and down the rope ladder (leading to the cage), thus giving the fans a chance to blow off steam. The ice would be marked off into numbered areas for face-offs and the referee would announce over the loudspeaker the reason for called penalties. One or two linesmen would be on the ice simply to handle faceoffs and get between fighters." Luckily, Ahearne's proposal was laughed out of the boardroom.

- In 1968, the IOC changed a rule in international hockey competition so that body checking was allowed in the offensive zone. Prior to this, players could hit only in the defensive zone.

- At the 1932 Winter Olympics in Lake Placid, New York, Canada had one of its best showings in an event, taking all the top three spots. Although dog-sledding was just a demonstration sport, Canadian canines made short work of the competition and easily walked away with the gold, silver and bronze. The canine gold-medal winners shared their prize with driver Emile St. Goddard.

- In curling, it is the pebbling of the ice that is responsible for that distinctive sound that all stones make as they travel down the ice. The rough bumpy surface creates friction between the stone and the ice, thereby making that familiar sound. If you listen carefully, it almost sounds as if the rock is saying, "Currrrrrrrllllllllll!" Almost.

- Not many athletes are able to train for two completely different sports for two major competitions at the same time, but Sue Halloway of Halifax, Nova Scotia, became the first Canadian athlete to compete in the Summer and Winter Games in the same year. At the 1976 Winter Olympics in Innsbruck, Austria, Galloway proudly represented her country in the cross-country relay race and then switched gears for the Summer Olympics in Montréal later that year to compete for her nation in the C-2 canoeing event. She did not win any medals at either Olympics.

- At the 1936 Winter Games in Garmisch-Partenkirchen, Germany, Canada sent 45-year-old Edwina Chamier to compete in the alpine skiing combined event. At 45 years and 318 days, she was the oldest competitor of the 20th century.

- At 39, Duff Gibson was the oldest Winter Olympic gold medallist in an individual event, in skeleton, at the 2006 Turin Games in Italy.

- At the 1948 Olympics in St. Moritz, Switzerland, Canada's Suzanne Morrow and her partner, Otto Diestelmeyer, became the first pair to perform the fabled death spiral in figure skating competition.

Their daring move catapulted them to a bronze-medal performance. The death spiral is performed when one partner (usually the man) braces himself with one skate in the ice and uses this skate as a pivot. He then grabs hold of his partner's hand, and she extends her body, circling around her partner with one blade touching the ice.

Stats

Canadian Medals by Sport: Winter Olympics

Sport	Gold	Silver	Bronze	Total
Alpine skiing	6	3	7	16
Biathlon	2	0	1	3
Bobsleigh	2	1	0	3
Cross-country skiing	2	1	0	3
Curling	2	2	2	6
Figure skating	3	7	10	20
Ice hockey	9	5	2	16
Speed skating— Long track/ Short track	11	18	19	48
Luge	0	0	0	0
Nordic combined	0	0	0	0
Skeleton	1	1	1	3
Ski jumping	0	0	0	0
Snowboard	1	0	1	2
Total	39	38	43	120

Winter Olympics Medals List—Canada

GOLD

Year	Name	Event
1920	Winnipeg Falcons: Robert Benson, Wally Byron, Frank Frederikson, Chris Fridfinnson, Mike Goodman, Haldor Halderson, Konrad Johannesson, Allan Woodman (*The Winter Games did not officially begin until 1924, but ice hockey was included in the 1920 Summer Games.*)	Hockey
1924	Toronto Granites: Jack Cameron, Ernie Collett, Albert McCaffery, Harold McMunn, Duncan Munro, W. Beattie Ramsay, Cyril Slater, Reg Smith, Harry Watson	Hockey
1928	University of Toronto Grads: Charles Delahay, Frank Fisher, Grant Gordon, Louis Hudson, Norbert Mueller, Bert Plaxton, Hugh Plaxton, Roger Plaxton, John Porter, Frank Sullivan, Joseph Sullivan, Ross Taylor, Dave Trottier	Hockey
1932	Winnipeg Hockey Club: William Cockburn, Cliff Crowley, Albert Duncanson,	Hockey

Medals List—Gold, cont'd

	George Garbutt, Roy Hinkel, Vic Lundquist, Norman Malloy, Walter Monson, Ken Moore, Romeo Rivers, Harold Simpson, Hugh Sutherland, Stan Wagner, Aliston Wise	
1936	*No gold medals*	
1940	*No Olympics due to WWII*	
1944	*No Olympics due to WWII*	
1948	Barbara Ann Scott	Figure skating
	RCAF Flyers: Hubert Brooks, Murray Dowey, Frank Dunster, Roy Forbes, Andrew Gilpin, Orval Gravelle, Patrick Guzzo, Wally Halder, Thomas Hibberd, Ross King, Andre Laperriere, Louis Lecompte, Julius (Pete) Leichnitz, George Mara, Albert Renaud, Reginald Schroeter, Irving Taylor	Hockey
1952	Edmonton Mercurys: George Abel, Jack Davies, Billie Dawe, Bruce Dickson, Don Gauf, Bill Gibson, Ralph Hansch, Bob Meyers, Dave Miller, Eric Paterson, Tom Pollock, Al Purvis, Gordie Robertson, Louis Secco, Frank Sullivan, Bob Watt	Hockey
1956	*No gold medals*	

Medals List—Gold, cont'd

1960	Anne Heggtveit	Alpine skiing—Slalom
	Barbara Wagner, Robert Paul	Figure skating—Pairs
1964	Douglas Anakin, John Emery, Vic Emery, Peter Kirby	Bobsleigh—4-man
1968	Nancy Greene	Alpine skiing—Giant slalom
1972	*No gold medals*	
1976	Kathy Kreiner	Alpine skiing—Giant slalom
1980	*No gold medals*	
1984	Gaetan Boucher	Speed skating—1000 m & 1500 m
1988	*No gold medals*	
1992	Angela Cutrone, Syvlie Daigle, Nathalie Lambert, Annie Perreault	Speed skating—Short track 3000-m relay
	Kerrin Lee-Gartner	Alpine skiing—Downhill
1994	Myriam Bedard	Biathlon—7.5 km & 15 km
	Jean-Luc Brassard	Freestyle skiing—Moguls
1998	Dave MacEacern, Pierre Lueders	Bobsleigh—2-man
	Sandra Schmirler, Marcia Gudereit, Joan McCusker, Jan Betker, Atina Ford	Curling

Medals List—Gold, cont'd

	Ross Rebagliati	Snowboarding— Giant slalom
	Catriona Le May Doan	Speed skating— 500 m
	Annie Perreault	Speed skating— Short track 500 m
	Francois Drolet, Marc Gagnon, Jonathon Guilmette, Eric Bedard, Derrick Campbell	Speed skating— Short track 5000-m relay
2002	Canada: Ed Belfour, Rob Blake, Eric Brewer, Martin Brodeur, Theoren Fleury, Adam Foote, Simon Gagne, Jarome Iginla, Curtis Joseph, Ed Jovanovski, Paul Kariya, Mario Lemieux, Eric Lindros, Al MacInnis, Scott Niedermayer, Joe Nieuwendyk, Owen Nolan, Michael Peca, Chris Pronger, Joe Sakic, Brendan Shanahan, Ryan Smyth, Steve Yzerman	Hockey
	Canada: Dana Antal, Kelly Bechard, Jennifer Botteril, Therese Brisson, Cassie Campbell, Isabelle Chartrand, Lori Dupuis, Danielle Goyette, Geraldine Heaney, Jayna Hefford, Becky Kellar, Caroline Ouellette, Cherie Piper,	Hockey

Medals List—Gold, cont'd

	Cheryl Pounder, Tammy Shewchuk, Samantha Small, Colleen Sostorics, Kim St. Pierre, Vicky Sunohara, Hayley Wickenheiser	
	Jamie Sale, David Pelletier	Figure skating—Pairs
	Catriona Le May Doan	Speed skating—500 m
	Beckie Scott	Cross-country skiing—10 km pursuit
	Marc Gagnon	Speed skating—Short track 500 m
	Eric Bedard, Marc Gagnon, Jonathan Guilmette, François-Louis Tremblay, Mathieu Turcotte	Speed skating—Short track 5000-m relay
2006	Chandra Crawford	Cross-country skiing—Sprint
	Brad Gushue, Jamie Korab, Russ Howard, Mark Nichols, Mike Adam	Curling
	Jennifer Heil	Freestyle skiing
	Canada: Meghan Agosta, Gillian Apps, Jennifer Botteril, Cassie Campbell, Gillian Ferrari, Danielle Goyette, Jayna Hefford, Becky Kellar,	Hockey

Medals List—Gold, cont'd

	Gina Kingsbury, Charline Labonte, Carla Labonte, Carla MacLeod, Caroline Ouellette, Cherie Piper, Cheryl Pounder, Colleen Sostorics, Kim St. Pierre, Vicky Sunohara, Sarah Vaillancourt, Katie Weatherston, Hayley Wickenheiser	
	Duff Gibson	Skeleton
	Cindy Klassen	Speed skating—1500 m
	Clara Hughes	Speed skating—5000 m

SILVER

Year	Name	Event
1924	*No silver medals*	
1928	*No silver medals*	
1932	Alex Hurd	Speed skating—1500 m
1936	Port Arthur Bear Cats: F. Maxwell Deacon, Ken Farmer, Hugh Farquharson, James Haggarty, Walter Kitchen, Ray Milton, Francis Moore, Herman Murray, Arthur Nash, Dave Neville, Ralph Saint-Germain, Alex Sinclair, William Thompson, N. Friday, G. Saxberg	Hockey

Medals List—Silver, cont'd

1940	No Olympics due to WWII	
1944	No Olympics due to WWII	
1948	No silver medals	
1952	No silver medals	
1956	Frances Dafoe, Norris Bowden	Figure skating—Pairs
1960	Kitchener-Waterloo Flying Dutchmen: Bobby Attersley, Maurice Benoit, James Connelly, Jack Douglas, Harold Hurley, Ken Laufmann, Floyd Martin, Robert McKnight, Cliff Pennington, Don Rope, Bobby Rousseau, George Samolenki, Harry Sinden, Darryl Sly	Hockey
1964	No silver medals	
1968	Nancy Greene	Alpine skiing—Slalom
1972	Karen Magnussen	Figure skating—Singles
1976	Cathy Priestner	Speed skating—500 m
1980	Gaetan Boucher	Speed skating—1000 m
1984	Brian Orser	Figure skating—Singles
1988	Brian Orser	Figure skating—Singles
	Elizabeth Manley	Figure skating—Singles

Medals List—Silver, cont'd

1992	Canada: Dave Archibald, Todd Brost, Sean Burke, Kevin Dahl, Curt Giles, Dave Hannan, Gord Hynes, Fabian Joseph, Joe Juneau, Trevor Kidd, Patrick Lebeau, Chris Lindberg, Eric Lindros, Kent Manderville, Adrien Plavsic, Dan Ratushny, Brad Schlegel, Wally Schreiber, Randy Smith, Sam St. Laurent, Dave Tippett, Brian Tutt, Jason Wooley	Hockey
	Frederic Blackburn	Speed skating— Short track 1000 m
	Frederic Blackburn, Laurent Daigneault, Michel Daignault, Sylvain Gagnon, Mark Lackie	Speed skating— Short track 5000-m relay
1994	Elvis Stojko	Figure skating— Singles
	Phillipe Laroche	Freestyle skiing— Aerials
	Canada: Mark Astley, Adri-anAucoin, David Harlock, Corey Hirsch, Todd Hlushko, Greg Johnson, Fabian Joseph, Paul Kariya, Chris Kontos, Manny Legace, Ken Lovsin, Derek Mayer, Pter Nedved, Dwayne Norris, Greg Parks,	Hockey

Medals List—Silver, cont'd

	Alain Roy, Jean-Yves Roy, Brian Savage, Brad Schlegel, Wally Schreiber, Chris Therien, Todd Warriner, Brad Werenka	
	Susan Auch	Speed skating— 500 m
	Nathalie Lambert	Speed skating— Short track 1000 m
	Christine Boudrias, Isabelle Charest, Sylvie Daigle, Nathalie Lambert	Speed skating— Short track 3000-m relay
1998	Jeremy Wotherspoon	Speed skating— 500 m
	Susan Auch	Speed skating— 500 m
	Elvis Stojko	Figure skating— Singles
	Mike Harris, Richard Hart, Collin Mitchell, George Karrys, Paul Savage	Curling
	Canada: Jennifer Botterill, Therese Brisson, Cassie Campbell, Judy Diduck, Nancy Drolet, Lori Dupuis, Danielle Goyette, Geraldine Heaney, Jayna Hefford, Becky Kellar, Kathy McCormack, Karen Nystrom, Lesley Reddon, Manon Rheaume,	Hockey

Medals List—Silver, cont'd

	Laura Schuler, Fiona Smith, France St. Louis, Vicky Sunohara, Hayley Wickenheiser, Stacy Wilson	
2002	Kevin Martin, Don Walchuk, Carter Rycroft, Don Barlett	Curling
	Jonathan Guillmette	Speed skating— 500 m
	Veronica Brenner	Freestyle skiing— Aerials
2006	Pierre Lueders, Lascelles Brown	Bobsleigh— 2-man
	Beckie Scott, Sara Renner	Cross-country skiing
	François-Louis Tremblay	Speed skating— Short track 500 m
	Eric Bedard, François-Louis Tremblay, Charles Hamelin, Mathieu Turcotte, Jonathan Guilmette	Speed skating— Short track 5000-m relay
	Alanna Kraus, Anouk Leblanc-Boucher, Kalyna Roberge, Tania Vicent, Amanda Overland	Speed skating— Short track 3000-m relay
	Jeff Pain	Skeleton
	Arne Dankers, Steven Elm, Denny Morrison, Jason Parker, Justin Warsylewicz	Speed skating— Team pursuit

Medals List—Silver, cont'd

	Kristina Groves, Clara Hughes, Cindy Klassen, Christine Nesbitt, Shannon Rempel	Speed skating— Team pursuit
	Cindy Klassen	Speed skating— 1000 m
	Kristina Groves	Speed skating— 1500 m

BRONZE

Year	Name	Event
1924	No bronze medals	
1928	No bronze medals	
1932	Montgomery Wilson	Figure skating— Singles
	Alex Hurd	Speed skating— 500 m
	William Logan	Speed skating— 1500 m & 5000 m
	Frank Stack	Speed skating— 10,000 m
1936	No bronze medals	
1940	No Olympics due to WWII	
1944	No Olympics due to WWII	
1948	Suzanne Morrow, Wallace Distelmeyer	Figure skating— Pairs
1952	Gordon Audley	Speed skating— 500 m

Medals List—Bronze, cont'd

1956	Lucile Wheeler	Alpine skiing—Downhill
	Kitchener-Waterloo Flying Dutchmen: Denis Brodeur, Charles Brooker, William Colvin, James Horne, Arthur Hurst, Byrle Klinck, Paul Knox, Ken Laufman, Howie Lee, James Logan, Floyd Martin, Jack MacKenzie, Don Rope, George Scholes, Gerry Theberge, Bob White, Keith Woodall	Hockey
1960	Donald Jackson	Figure skating—Singles
1964	Debbie Wilkes, Guy Revell	Figure skating—Pairs
	Petra Burka	Figure skating—Singles
1968	Team Canada: Roger Bourbonnais, Ken Broderick, Ray Cadieux, Paul Conlin, Gary Dineen, Brian Glennie, Ted Hargreaves, Fran Huck, Marshall Johnston, Barry MacKenzie, Billy McMillan, Steve Monteith, Morris Mott, Terry O'Malley, Herb Onder, Danny O'Shea, Gerry Pinder, Wayne Stephenson	Hockey

Medals List—Bronze, cont'd

1972	No bronze medals	
1976	Toller Cranston	Figure skating—Singles
1980	Steve Podborski	Alpine skiing—Downhill
1984	Gaetan Boucher	Speed skating—500 m
1988	Karen Percy	Alpine skiing—Downhill & Super-G
	Tracy Wilson, Rob McCall	Figure skating—Dance
1992	Myriam Bedard	Biathlon
	Isabelle Brasseur, Lloyd Eisler	Figure skating—Pairs
1994	Edi Podivinsky	Alpine skiing—Downhill
	Isabelle Brasseur, Lloyd Eisler	Figure skating—Pairs
	Lloyd Langlois	Freestyle skiing—Aerials
	Marc Gagnon	Speed skating—Short track 1000 m
1998	Kevin Overland	Speed skating—500 m
	Eric Bedard	Speed skating—Short track 1000 m

Medals List—Bronze, cont'd

	Christine Boudrias, Isabelle Charest, Annie Perreault, Tania Vincent	Speed skating— Short track 3000-m relay
	Catriona Le May Doan	Speed skating— 1000 m
2002	Marc Gagnon	Speed skating— Short track 1500 m
	Kelly Law, Julie Skinner, Georgina Wheatcraft, Diane Nelson	Curling
	Deidra Dionne	Freestyle skiing— Aerials
	Cindy Klassen	Speed skating— 3000 m
	Clara Hughes	Speed skating— 5000 m
	Mathieu Turcotte	Speed skating— Short track 1000 m
	Alana Kraus, Marie-Eve Drolet, Amelie Goulet-Nadon, Isabelle Charest	Speed skating— Short track 3000-m relay
2006	Shannon Kleibrink, Amy Nixon, Glenys Bakker, Christine Keshen, Sandra Jenkins	Curling
	Jeffrey Buttle	Figure skating— Singles

Medals List—Bronze, cont'd

	Anouk Leblanc-Boucher	Speed skating—Short track 500 m
	Mellisa Hollingsworth	Skeleton
	Dominique Maltais	Snowboarding—Cross
	Cindy Klassen	Speed skating—3000 m & 5000 m

Flag Bearers for the Winter Olympics

Year	City	Flag Bearer	Sport
1924	Chamonix	Ernie Collett	Hockey
1928	St. Moritz	John Porter	Hockey
1932	Lake Placid	Multiple	
1936	Garmisch	Multiple	
1940	*No Olympics due to WWII*		
1944	*No Olympics due to WWII*		
1948	St. Moritz	Hubert Brooks	Hockey
1952	Oslo	Gordon Audley	Speed skating
1956	Cortina	Norris Bowden	Figure skating
1960	Squaw Valley	Robert Paul	Figure skating
1964	Innsbruck	Ralph Olin	Speed skating
1968	Grenoble	Nancy Greene	Alpine skiing
1972	Sapporo	Karen Magnussen	Figure skating
1976	Innsbruck	Dave Irwin	Alpine skiing
1980	Lake Placid	Ken Read	Alpine skiing
1984	Sarajevo	Gaetan Boucher	Speed skating
1988	Calgary	Brian Orser	Figure skating

1992	Albertville	Sylvie Daigle	Speed skating
1994	Lillehammer	Kurt Browning	Figure skating
1998	Nagano	Jean-Luc Brassard	Freestyle skiing
2002	Salt Lake City	Catriona Le May Doan	Speed skating
2006	Turin	Danielle Goyette	Hockey

Canadian Athletes to Watch in 2010

Alpine Skiing	Emily Brydon
	Robbie Dixon
	Erik Guay
	Jan Hudec
	Britt Janyk
	Michael Janyk
	Manuel Osborne-Paradis
	Larisa Yurkiw

Biathlon	Zina Kocher
	Jean Philippe Le Guellec

Bobsleigh	Shelley-Ann Brown
	Jenny Ciochetti
	Kaillie Humphries
	Pierre Lueders
	Heather Moyse
	Helen Upperton

Figure Skating	Craig Buntin
	Patrick Chan
	Vanessa Crone
	Bryce Davison
	Jessica Dubé

	Meaghan Duhamel
	Cody Hay
	Anabelle Langlois
	Scott Moir
	Cynthia Phaneuf
	Paul Poirier
	Joannie Rochette
	Shawn Sawyer
	Tessa Virtue

Hockey (Women)	Gillian Apps
	Jennifer Botterill
	Jayna Hefford
	Rebecca Johnston
	Gina Kingsbury
	Marie-Philip Poulin
	Sarah Vaillancourt
	Jennifer Wakefield
	Hayley Wickenheiser

Hockey (Men) (as of this writing)	Goaltender	Martin Brodeur
		Roberto Luongo
		Steve Mason
		Cam Ward
	Defense	Jay Bouwmeester
		Dan Boyle
		Brent Burns

		Mike Green
		Duncan Keith
		Scott Niedermayer
		Dion Phaneuf
		Chris Pronger
		Robyn Regehr
		Shea Weber
	Forward	Jeff Carter
		Sidney Crosby
		Shane Doan
		Simon Gagne
		Ryan Getzlaf
		Dany Heatley
		Jarome Iginla
		Vincent Lecavalier
		Brendan Morrow
		Rick Nash
		Corey Perry
		Mike Richards
		Joe Sakic
		Marc Savard
		Martin St. Louis
		Eric Staal
		Jonathan Toews
	Head Coach	Mike Babcock

Luge	Jeff Christie
	Alex Gough

	Regan Lauscher
	Chris Moffat
	Mike Moffat
	Meaghan Simister

Short Track Speed Skating	Michael Gilday
	Charles Hamelin
	Francois Hamelin
	Kalyna Roberge
	François Louis Tremblay

Ski Jumping	Trevor Morrice
	Stefan Read

Long Track Speed Skating	Kristina Groves
	Clara Hughes
	Cindy Klassen
	Denny Morrison
	Jeremy Wotherspoon

Cross-country Skiing	Ivan Babikov
	Chandra Crawford
	Drew Goldsack
	George Grey
	Alex Harvey

	Perianne Jones
	Devon Kershaw
	Sara Renner
	Phillip Widmer

Curling	Glenn Howard
	Jennifer Jones
	Kevin Martin

Freestyle Skiing	Davey Barr
	Nathalie Bazin
	Alexandre Bilodeau
	Jackie Brown
	Aleisha Cline
	Chris Del Bosco
	Deidra Dionne
	Chloe Dufour-Lapointe
	Maxime Dufour-Lapointe
	Stanley Hayer
	Jenn Heil
	Ashleigh McIvor
	Steve Omischl
	Amber Peterson
	Kristi Richards

Nordic Combined	Jason Myslicki
	Wesley Savill

Skeleton	Paul Boehm
	Mike Douglas
	Kelly Forbes
	Mellisa Hollingsworth
	Michelle Kelly
	Keith Loach
	Jon Montgomery
	Jeff Pain
	Carla Pavan
	Sarah Reid

Snowboarding	Jasey-Jay Anderson
	Dominque Maltais
	Matthew Morison

Notes on Sources

Best, Dave. (ed.) *Canada: Our Century in Sport.* Markham: Fitzhenry & Whiteside, 2002.

Black, Rod. *Lillehammer '94: Canada's Olympic Stories.* Toronto: Infact Publishing, 1994.

Judd, Ron C. *The Winter Olympics.* Seattle: The Mountaineers Books, 2008.

MacGregor, Roy. *A Loonie for Luck.* Toronto: McClelland & Stewart, 2002.

Podnieks, Andrew. *Canada's Olympic Hockey Teams.* Toronto: Doubleday Canada Ltd., 1997.

Wallechinsky, David, and Jaime Loucky. *The Complete Book of the Winter Olympics.* Toronto: Sports Media Publishing, 2005.

Web Sources

CTV
http://www.ctvolympics.ca/ (accessed April 15 to May 20, 2009).

Database Olympics
http://www.databaseolympics.com/ (accessed from April 15 to May 20, 2009).

Canadian Broadcasting Corporation
http://www.cbc.ca/news/story/2007/02/12/vancouver-countdown.html

http://www.cbc.ca/canada/british-columbia/
story/2009/05/18/bc-sex-worker-training.html
http://www.cbc.ca/canada/british-columbia/
story/2007/05/08/bc-atlanta.html
http://www.cbc.ca/sports/hockey/story/2008/10/17/
steve-yzerman.html (accessed from April 15 to
May 20, 2009).

Hockey Canada
http://www.hockeycanada.ca/index.php/ci_id/57519/
la_id/1.htm (accessed from April 15 to May 20, 2009).

Skate Canada
http://www.skatecanada.ca/en/about_skate_canada/
history/, http://www.skatecanada.ca/en/news_views/
press_room/news_releases/2009/?CFID=9996792&
CFTOKEN=55118222 (accessed from April 15 to
May 20, 2009).

Freestyle Ski Canada
http://www.freestyleski.ca/en/archives/ (accessed
from April 15 to May 20, 2009).

Canski
http://www.canski.org/webconcepteur/web/alpine
(accessed from April 15 to May 20, 2009).

J. Alexander Poulton

J. Alexander Poulton is a writer, photographer and genuine Canadian sports enthusiast. A resident of Montréal all his life, he has been known to "call in sick" during the Olympics broadcast so that he can get as much viewing in as possible.

He earned his B.A in English Literature from McGill University and his graduate diploma in Journalism from Concordia University. He has 10 other sports books to his credit, including books on hockey, soccer and baseball.